Build a WordPress WooCommerce From Scratch

2023
Raphael Heide

Build a WordPress WooCommerce From Scratch
Published by raphaelheide.com
Copyright ® 2023

Heide, Raphael 2023 Buil a WordPress WooCommerce From Scratch

THANK YOU TO MY READERS

I appreciate that there are many resources available, and I am genuinely grateful that you have chosen our book as your learning tool for building your WordPress website. My objective is to provide you with a comprehensive and up-to-date guide that empowers you to create impressive websites confidently and effortlessly.

I sincerely hope that the knowledge and techniques shared in the book have proven valuable in your pursuit of building your dream website. I understand that website creation can be intricate, but I have worked hard to make it accessible to beginners and experienced users alike. Your dedication to learning and growth is commendable, and I am excited to be a part of your journey.

I would also like to express my heartfelt gratitude to those who have reached out with questions, feedback, and suggestions. Your engagement and interaction mean the world to me. I am constantly seeking ways to improve and enhance our content, and your input helps me deliver a more enriching experience to all our readers.

Furthermore, I invite you to stay connected with me. If you have any further questions, need additional guidance, or simply want to share your success stories, please feel free to reach out. Your continued support is highly valued, and I am dedicated to assisting you in your WordPress website endeavors.

Once again, thank you for being a part of our readership. Your enthusiasm and dedication inspire me to continue creating valuable content and empowering individuals like you to achieve their website-building goals. I wish you ongoing success and fulfillment in all your future endeavors.

Warm regards,

Raphael Heide

INTRODUCTION

Welcome to "How to Build a WordPress WooCommerce from Scratch"! In this book, we will guide you through the process of creating your very own WooCommerce store using WordPress, from the ground up. Whether you're a budding entrepreneur, a small business owner, or an individual looking to start an online business, this book aims to provide you with the knowledge and tools necessary to create a successful e-commerce store.

My name is Raphael Heide, a WordPress developer and I will delve into the reasons why this book is a valuable resource for anyone interested in building a WooCommerce store from scratch. I understand that starting an online business can be overwhelming, especially if you're new to the world of e-commerce. This book is designed to simplify the process and empower you with the necessary skills to navigate the challenges of building a WooCommerce store.

WordPress is a popular content management system (CMS) that powers millions of websites worldwide. Its user-friendly interface and extensive plugin ecosystem make it an ideal choice for building various types of websites. WooCommerce, on the other hand, is a powerful e-commerce plugin for WordPress that enables you to transform your website into a fully functional online store.

Together we will explore the features and capabilities of both WordPress and WooCommerce, highlighting their strengths and explaining how they work together to create a robust e-commerce platform. By understanding the fundamentals of these tools, you'll be better equipped to leverage their potential and make informed decisions throughout the store-building process.

Building a WooCommerce store from scratch offers several benefits that are worth considering.

Customization and Control: Creating a WooCommerce store from scratch gives you complete control over the design, layout, and functionality of your website. You can tailor every aspect to align with your brand identity and business goals. This level of customization allows for a unique and memorable user experience, setting you apart from competitors using pre-built templates.

Scalability and Flexibility: By starting from scratch, you have the opportunity to design a store that can grow and adapt as your business expands. You can implement scalable infrastructure, optimize performance, and integrate new features and functionalities seamlessly. This flexibility ensures that your store can keep up with evolving market trends and customer demands.

Cost-effectiveness: Building a WooCommerce store from scratch can be a cost-effective approach compared to hiring a web developer or opting for a fully custom-built solution. While there may be initial investment involved, the long-term savings and control over expenses can be significant.

Learning and Empowerment: Embarking on the journey of building your WooCommerce store from scratch allows you to acquire valuable skills and knowledge. You'll gain a deeper understanding of how e-commerce works, enhance your problem-solving abilities, and develop the confidence to manage and maintain your store independently.

Adaptability and Integration: WooCommerce seamlessly integrates with numerous plugins and extensions, offering extensive functionality options. By building your store from scratch, you can selectively choose and integrate the tools and extensions that best suit your business needs, ensuring a tailored and cohesive ecosystem.

By recognizing these benefits, you'll be motivated and equipped to embark on the exciting journey of building your own WooCommerce store from scratch. Throughout this book, we will guide you step-by-step, providing detailed instructions, best practices, and tips to help you navigate the process with confidence.

So, grab your favorite beverage, find a cozy spot, and embark on this exciting adventure of mastering WordPress. Get ready to unleash your creativity, build impressive websites, and tap into the vast potential of the WordPress ecosystem. Let's dive in and make the most of this incredible resource!

SUMMARY

UNDERSTANDING WORDPRESS AND WOOCOMMERCE

Before we delve into the intricacies of WooCommerce, it's essential to understand the foundation on which it is built - WordPress. WordPress has come a long way since its inception in 2003 as a simple blogging platform. Over the years, it has evolved into a robust content management system (CMS) that powers millions of websites across various industries.

Originally developed by Matt Mullenweg and Mike Little, WordPress was created with the goal of democratizing publishing, making it accessible to anyone with a computer and an internet

WORDPRESS

connection. It gained popularity for its user-friendly interface, extensive customization options, and a vibrant community that contributed to its growth.

EXPLORING THE WORDPRESS CMS

WordPress operates on a PHP and MySQL framework and is known for its simplicity, versatility, and scalability. The CMS provides users with an intuitive dashboard where they can create, manage, and publish content without the need for programming knowledge.

With its vast ecosystem of themes and plugins, WordPress allows users to customize their websites and add advanced functionalities with ease.

The key components of WordPress include:

Themes: WordPress offers a wide range of themes that determine the overall design and layout of your website. Themes can be customized to align with your brand identity, ensuring a unique online presence.

Plugins: Plugins are add-ons that extend the functionality of your WordPress website. They enable you to add features such as contact forms, SEO optimization, e-commerce capabilities, and more. With thousands of free and premium plugins available, you can enhance your website's capabilities without the need for custom development.

Content Creation and Management: WordPress provides a powerful yet user-friendly content editor known as the Gutenberg editor. It allows you to create and organize your content efficiently, incorporating multimedia elements and structuring your website's pages and posts.

THE WOOCOMMERCE HISTORY

WooCommerce, originally developed by WooThemes, emerged in 2011 as a plugin designed to add e-commerce functionality to WordPress websites. It gained rapid popularity due to its seamless integration with WordPress, robust feature set, and user-friendly interface.

WooCommerce was acquired by Automattic, the company behind WordPress.com, in 2015. This acquisition further solidified WooCommerce's position as the go-to e-commerce solution for

WordPress users. Today, WooCommerce powers a significant portion of online stores, ranging from small businesses to large enterprises.

INTRODUCTION TO WOOCOMMERCE AND ITS FEATURES

WooCommerce empowers website owners to transform their WordPress websites into fully functional e-commerce stores. It provides a comprehensive set of features that enable you to sell products, manage inventory, process payments, and more.

Key features of WooCommerce include:

Product Management: WooCommerce allows you to add and manage products effortlessly. You can create product variations, set prices, configure stock levels, define shipping options, and customize product attributes.

Payment Gateways: With WooCommerce, you can integrate various payment gateways to process transactions securely. Popular options include PayPal, Stripe, Square, and more. These gateways support a wide range of payment methods, ensuring convenience for your customers.

Shipping Options: WooCommerce offers flexible shipping options, enabling you to define shipping zones, rates, and methods. You can set up flat rates, weight-based rates, or integrate with shipping carriers for real-time shipping calculations.

Extensibility through Plugins: Just like WordPress, WooCommerce has a vast ecosystem of plugins that extend its functionality. You can enhance your store with plugins for marketing, analytics, customer management, advanced product options, and more.

Reporting and Analytics: WooCommerce provides built-in reporting and analytics features that allow you to track sales, monitor inventory, analyze customer behavior, and gain valuable insights to optimize your store's performance.

By understanding the history and features of both WordPress

and WooCommerce, you are equipped with the foundational knowledge necessary to leverage these powerful tools. In the subsequent chapters, we will dive deeper into the process of setting up and customizing your WooCommerce store, empowering you to create a successful online business.

_____ NOTE _____

You can check my book Build a WordPress Website From Scratch 2024". It's a great tool to start make your website from scratch.

YOUR DOMAIN

In today's digital age, owning a domain name is essential for establishing a strong online presence. A domain name serves as the unique address of your website, making it easier for visitors to find and access your content. Whether you're creating a personal blog, an e-commerce store, or a business website, having your own domain name offers numerous advantages.

One of the primary benefits of owning a domain name is the professional and credible image it portrays for your online identity. Instead of relying on free subdomains or lengthy URLs, having a custom domain name gives your website a polished and professional touch. It enhances your brand recognition and helps build trust among your audience by conveying a sense of authenticity and legitimacy.

When it comes to the cost of a domain name, it can vary depending on several factors. The price is influenced by the top-level domain (TLD) you choose, such as .com, .org, .net, and others. The domain registrar you use and any additional services or features you opt for can also impact the cost. On average, a domain name typically ranges from $10 to $20 per year. However, premium or highly sought-after domain names may command higher prices.

It's important to note that domain name pricing may vary between countries and registrars. Some TLDs may have higher costs than others, especially if they are in high demand. It's worth exploring different options and comparing prices to find the best deal for your desired domain name. Additionally, keep in mind that some domain registrars may offer promotional discounts or bundle deals, providing further opportunities to save money.

When selecting a domain name, consider choosing one that reflects your brand, is easy to remember, and aligns with the purpose of your website. Conduct thorough research to ensure that your desired domain name is available and not trademarked by someone else. This step is crucial in securing a domain name that accurately represents your online identity.

Uniform Resource Locator(URL)

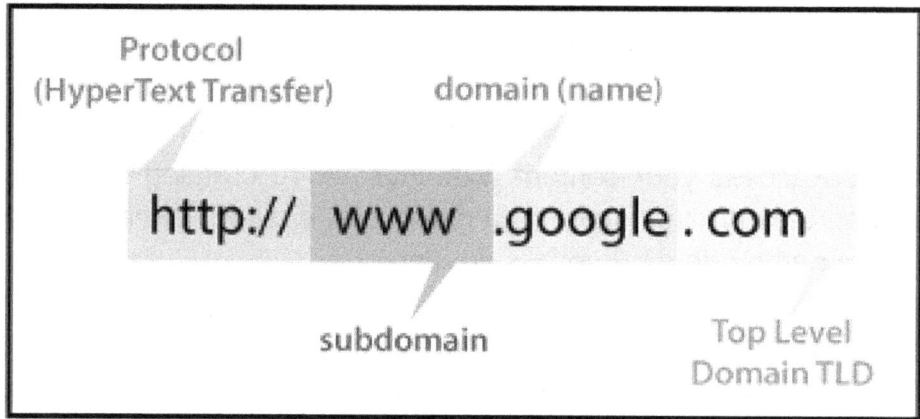

Now, let's discuss why it is important to have your own domain:

Branding and Credibility: A domain name that aligns with your company or personal brand enhances your credibility and professionalism. It creates a memorable and unique online identity that visitors can associate with your business or personal endeavors.

Customization and Control: Owning your domain gives you complete control over your website and email addresses. You can customize the domain name to align with your brand, choose the desired extensions (such as .com, .org, or .net), and create personalized email addresses (e.g., info@ yourdomain.com).

Consistency and Longevity: Having your own domain ensures consistency in your online presence. Unlike social media platforms or free website hosting services, which can change their policies or shut down, a domain provides a stable and long-term online address that you can rely on.

Search Engine Visibility: A domain that incorporates relevant keywords can improve your search engine rankings. When users search for specific products, services, or information related to your domain, having a well-optimized website can increase your visibility and attract organic traffic.

Professional Email Communication: With a domain, you can create email addresses that match your domain name, such as yourname@yourdomain.com. This adds a professional touch to your communication and strengthens your brand image.

Now that you understand the importance of having your own domain, let's explore where you can register domains:

Domain Registrars: Domain registrars are companies authorized to sell domain names. They provide registration services, domain management tools, and customer support. Popular domain registrars include GoDaddy, Namecheap, and Google Domains.

Web Hosting Providers: Many web hosting providers offer domain registration services as part of their hosting packages. This option is convenient if you plan to host your website with the same provider. Examples of hosting providers that offer domain registration include Bluehost, SiteGround, and DreamHost.

Country-Specific Registrars: Some countries have specific registrars for their top-level domain extensions. For instance, if you want a .uk domain, you can register it through the UK registry, Nominet. It's advisable to use country-specific registrars for localized businesses or organizations.

Resellers and Marketplaces: Various resellers and marketplaces exist where you can register domains. These platforms often provide competitive pricing and additional services. Examples include Sedo, Flippa, and BuyDomains.

Domain Auctions and Expired Domains Marketplaces:

Domain auctions and expired domains marketplaces allow you to bid or purchase domains that have been previously registered but are now available. These platforms, such as GoDaddy Auctions and NameJet, can be an option if you're looking for premium or highly sought-after domain names.

When choosing a domain registrar, consider a few factors:

Pricing: Compare the registration fees and renewal costs to ensure they fit your budget.

Domain Extensions: Check the registrar's available domain extensions and their pricing, as some extensions may be more expensive than others.

Domain Management Tools: Evaluate the domain management features provided by the registrar, such as DNS management, domain forwarding, and privacy protection.

Customer Support: Look for a registrar with reliable customer support, as you may need assistance with domain configuration or troubleshooting.

Registering your own domain is crucial for establishing a professional online presence and maintaining control over your brand and website. It offers branding opportunities, customization, search engine visibility, and professional email communication.

Carefully consider your requirements and choose a registrar that offers competitive pricing, domain management tools, and reliable customer support to make the most out of your domain registration experience.

YOUR WEB HOSTING

Web hosting is a crucial aspect of establishing your online presence. It involves renting server space and resources to store and make your website accessible on the internet. The significance of web hosting can be understood through the following points:

Website Performance: The speed, performance, and reliability of your website depend on your web hosting provider. A reputable provider ensures that your website loads quickly and remains accessible, providing visitors with a smooth user experience.

Storage and Bandwidth: Web hosting offers storage space for your website files, databases, images, and other content. It also provides bandwidth, which determines the amount of data transferred between your website and its visitors. Adequate storage and bandwidth are essential for accommodating website growth and handling increased traffic.

Customization and Control: With web hosting, you have complete control over your website's configuration, design, and functionality. You can install and customize content management systems like WordPress, Joomla, or Drupal, and integrate various plugins, themes, and extensions to enhance your website's features and appearance.

Email Hosting: Many web hosting providers offer email hosting services, enabling you to create professional email addresses using your domain name. This fosters a cohesive brand identity and facilitates effective communication with your audience.

Security and Backup: Web hosting companies implement security measures to protect your website from cyber threats such as malware, hacking attempts, and DDoS attacks. Additionally, they often provide regular backups, ensuring that your website's data can be restored in case of any unforeseen issues or data loss.

SOME EXAMPLES OF WEB HOSTING PROVIDERS

Bluehost: A well-known provider recommended by WordPress.org, offering reliable performance, 24/7 customer support, and user-friendly control panels.

SiteGround: Known for excellent customer support and robust security features, providing shared hosting, cloud hosting, and dedicated servers.

HostGator: A popular choice for beginners with affordable shared hosting plans, offering a drag-and-drop website builder, one-click WordPress installation, and various hosting options.

DreamHost: Offers shared hosting, managed WordPress hosting, VPS, and dedicated servers, focusing on reliable performance, solid security features, and extensive developer tools.

WP Engine: Specializes in managed WordPress hosting, providing robust security, automatic backups, staging environments, and excellent customer support tailored to WordPress users.

When selecting a web hosting provider, consider factors such as hosting plans, pricing, reliability and uptime guarantees, customer support, and the user-friendliness of the control panel. By carefully evaluating these factors and choosing a reputable web hosting provider, you can establish a solid foundation for your website's success.

SETTING UP YOUR HOSTING AND DOMAIN

Configuring the Domain Name System (DNS) settings for your domain is an important step after registering your domain and acquiring web hosting. DNS translates human-readable domain names into IP addresses used by computers to locate your website. In this chapter, we will walk you through the process of configuring DNS and discuss the concept of propagation time.

To access DNS settings, follow these steps:

- Log in to your domain registrar's website, where you registered your domain.

- Locate the domain management section or domain settings for the specific domain you want to configure.

- Look for options such as "DNS Management," "Name Servers," or "DNS Settings," which may vary depending on your registrar.

Name servers store DNS records for your domain. By default, your domain registrar assigns their own name servers to your domain. However, if you have web hosting, you need to update the name servers to point to your hosting provider's name servers.

Here's how:

- Obtain the name server information from your web hosting provider, usually two or more name server addresses.

- In the DNS settings of your domain registrar, locate the name server fields.

- Replace the existing name server addresses with the ones provided by your web hosting provider.

- Save the changes.

DNS propagation refers to the time it takes for updated DNS information to propagate across the internet. During this period, different DNS servers worldwide update their records. Propagation is not immediate and can take minutes to 48 hours or more.

Due to the variation in DNS server update intervals, some users may still see the old DNS records, while others will see the updated information. It's important to understand propagation time and be patient while waiting for the changes to take effect.

Check your DNS: search online for DNS Propagation and check a free online website. Or just check online in whatsmydns.net

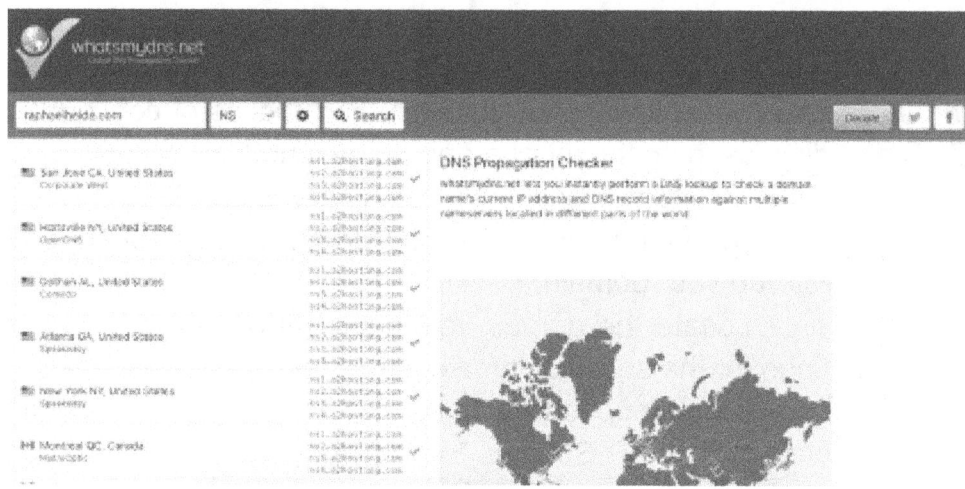

TO VERIFY DNS CONFIGURATION, YOU CAN PERFORM THE FOLLOWING CHECKS

Use DNS lookup tools online to perform DNS lookups for your domain. Compare the returned information with your updated DNS settings.

Clear your computer and internet service provider's DNS cache to ensure it fetches the updated records. Clearing cache instructions depend on your operating system.

In addition to name server updates, you may need to configure other DNS records based on your website's requirements. Common

DNS records include:

A Record: Associates your domain name with the IP address of your web hosting server.

CNAME Record: Allows you to create subdomains or alias domains that point to another domain or server.

MX Record: Specifies the mail server responsible for handling email delivery for your domain.

SPF Record: Helps prevent email spoofing and verifies legitimate emails sent from your domain.

TXT Record: Lets you add custom text-based information to your DNS records, often used for verification or providing additional details.

Consult your web hosting provider's documentation or support resources to understand specific DNS records you may need to configure.

Once DNS configuration is complete and changes have propagated, your domain will be properly connected to your web hosting. Periodically review and update DNS settings as needed, especially when making changes to your hosting provider or server configuration.

INSTALLING WORDPRESS

After successfully registering your domain, configuring DNS, and acquiring web hosting, the next step is to install WordPress, a widely used content management system that empowers numerous websites globally. In this chapter, we will provide you with a step-by-step guide on how to install WordPress on your chosen web host.

Before proceeding with the installation, ensure that you have the following information readily available:

Access to your web hosting account: This includes your hosting provider's login credentials and the necessary details to access your hosting control panel.

Domain name: The domain you registered will be used for your WordPress website.

Let's now dive into the process of installing WordPress:

Access your hosting control panel: Log in to your web hosting account and locate the control panel, which is often provided through platforms like cPanel, Plesk, or a custom interface offered by your hosting provider.

Find the "Auto Installer" or "One-Click Installer" option: Most hosting control panels include an auto installer utility that simplifies the WordPress installation process. Look for an icon or link labeled "Auto Installer" or "One-Click Installer" within your control panel.

Select WordPress as your installation option: Once you locate the installer, click on it to initiate the installation process. You will likely be presented with a list of applications, and you should choose WordPress from the available options.

Configure installation settings: After selecting WordPress, you will be prompted to configure various installation settings. These typically include selecting your domain name, entering a desired username and password for your WordPress admin account, and providing an email address associated with your website.

Start the installation: Once you've entered the necessary information, click on the "Install" or "Start" button to begin the installation process. The installer will take care of copying the required files and setting up the WordPress database for your website.

Wait for the installation to complete: The installer will display a progress bar or notification indicating the status of the installation. Depending on your hosting provider and server resources, the installation process may take a few moments.

Access your WordPress website: Once the installation is complete, you will receive a confirmation message with the URL and login details for your WordPress admin panel. Take note of this information as it will be essential for managing your website.

_____ NOTE _____

If you want a comprehensive guide that explains the basics and provides a step-by-step manual installation of WordPress, I recommend the book "Build a WordPress Website From Scratch 2024." This book will walk you through the entire process of setting up a WordPress website, starting from the installation phase. With detailed instructions and explanations, it will equip you with the knowledge and skills needed to create your own WordPress site.

CONFIGURING WORDPRESS SETTINGS

In this chapter, we will delve into the process of configuring WordPress settings to optimize your website's functionality and appearance. WordPress offers a wide range of settings that allow you to customize various aspects of your website, from general site information to user roles and permalinks. By understanding and adjusting these settings, you can ensure that your WordPress site is tailored to your specific needs.

First step: you need to login your WordPress Panel: yousite. com/wp-admin

GENERAL SETTINGS

The General Settings section is where you can configure basic information about your website. To access these settings, navigate to the WordPress dashboard and click on "Settings" in the left-hand menu, followed by "General." Here, you can set your site title, tagline, and email address associated with the site. You can also choose whether to display your website as www or non-www and set the time zone.

WRITING SETTINGS

The Writing Settings section allows you to define default settings for creating and publishing posts. Within this section, you can specify the default category and post format, as well as enable features like the post via email or remote publishing.

Additionally, you can configure the settings for the built-in WordPress editor, such as the size of the post box and the formatting options available.

READING SETTINGS

The Reading Settings section determines how your website's content is displayed to visitors. Here, you can choose whether to display your latest posts or a static page as the homepage. You can also set the number of posts displayed on each page and configure options related to RSS feeds and search engine visibility.

DISCUSSION SETTINGS

The Discussion Settings section allows you to control how comments are managed on your WordPress site. You can choose whether to enable or disable comments on your posts and pages, set comment moderation rules, and configure options for email notifications and avatars. Additionally, you can manage settings related to pingbacks and trackbacks.

MEDIA SETTINGS

The Media Settings section enables you to define the default sizes for images uploaded to your WordPress site. You can specify the dimensions for thumbnail, medium, and large images, as well as set the quality level for image compression. These settings help ensure that your media files are appropriately sized and optimized for display on your website.

PERMALINK SETTINGS

Permalinks are the permanent URLs that point to your individual posts, pages, and other content on your website. The Permalink Settings section allows you to define the structure of your permalinks. WordPress offers several options for permalink structures, including a plain format, date-based formats, and custom structures that include post names or category slugs. Choosing a descriptive and SEO-friendly permalink structure is important for search engine visibility and user experience.

PRIVACY SETTINGS

The Privacy Settings section provides options for configuring your website's privacy policy. You can specify a privacy policy page or create a new one, which is essential for compliance with data protection regulations such as the General Data Protection Regulation (GDPR). Including a privacy policy on your site helps inform visitors about the data you collect and how it is used.

USER ROLES AND PERMISSIONS

WordPress offers a robust system for managing user roles and permissions. By default, there are several user roles with different levels of access and capabilities, including Administrator, Editor, Author, Contributor, and Subscriber. In the User Roles and

Permissions settings, you can define the capabilities assigned to each user role or create custom roles with specific permissions tailored to your needs.

Configuring these WordPress settings allows you to personalize and optimize your website's functionality and user experience. By exploring each section and adjusting the settings according to your preferences and requirements, you can ensure that your WordPress site is set up to meet your specific goals and deliver a seamless experience to your visitors.

_____ NOTE _____

If you want a comprehensive guide that explains the basics and provides a step-by-step manual installation of WordPress, I recommend the book "Build a WordPress Website From Scratch 2024." The book will walk you through the entire process of setting up a WordPress website, starting from the installation phase. With detailed instructions and explanations, it will equip you with the knowledge and skills needed to create your own WordPress site.

CHOOSING AND INSTALLING A WOOCOMMERCE-COMPATIBLE THEME

In this chapter, we will explore the process of selecting and installing a WooCommerce-compatible theme for your WordPress website. WooCommerce is a popular e-commerce plugin for WordPress that allows you to create and manage an online store. Choosing the right theme is crucial to ensure that your store has a visually appealing design, user-friendly interface, and seamless integration with WooCommerce's features.

THEME SELECTION CRITERIA

When choosing a WooCommerce-compatible theme, consider the following criteria to ensure that it meets your specific requirements:

Design and Layout: Look for a theme that aligns with your brand identity and offers a visually appealing design. Consider the layout options available, such as the number of columns, product showcase areas, and customization possibilities.

Responsiveness: With the increasing use of mobile devices, it's essential to select a theme that is responsive and provides a seamless browsing experience across different screen sizes. Ensure that the theme is optimized for mobile and offers a mobile-friendly design.

WooCommerce Integration: Verify that the theme explicitly states its compatibility with WooCommerce. It should have dedicated WooCommerce templates and styling to ensure a cohesive and integrated look for your online store.

Customization Options: Assess the theme's customization options and flexibility. Look for themes that offer easy customization through built-in options or integration with popular page builders. This allows you to personalize the appearance of your store without coding knowledge.

Performance: A fast-loading website is crucial for user experience and search engine optimization. Check if the theme is optimized for speed and performance by reading reviews or testing it with tools like Google PageSpeed Insights or GTmetrix.

Support and Updates: Ensure that the theme is actively maintained and supported by its developers. Regular updates ensure compatibility with the latest versions of WordPress and WooCommerce, as well as security patches and bug fixes. Look for themes with good customer support and documentation.

SOME WOOCOMMERCE THEMES

Choosing the best WordPress theme for WooCommerce largely depends on your specific needs, preferences, and the type of online store you want to create. However, there are several popular themes known for their compatibility with WooCommerce and their extensive features. Here are some of the top WooCommerce themes to consider:

Storefront: Developed by WooCommerce's parent company, Storefront is a free theme specifically designed for WooCommerce. It offers a clean and minimalist design, easy customization options, and seamless integration with WooCommerce's features. Storefront is highly recommended for beginners and can be enhanced with additional Storefront child themes and extensions.

Divi: Divi is a highly versatile and widely used theme that comes with its own page builder, making it easy to create

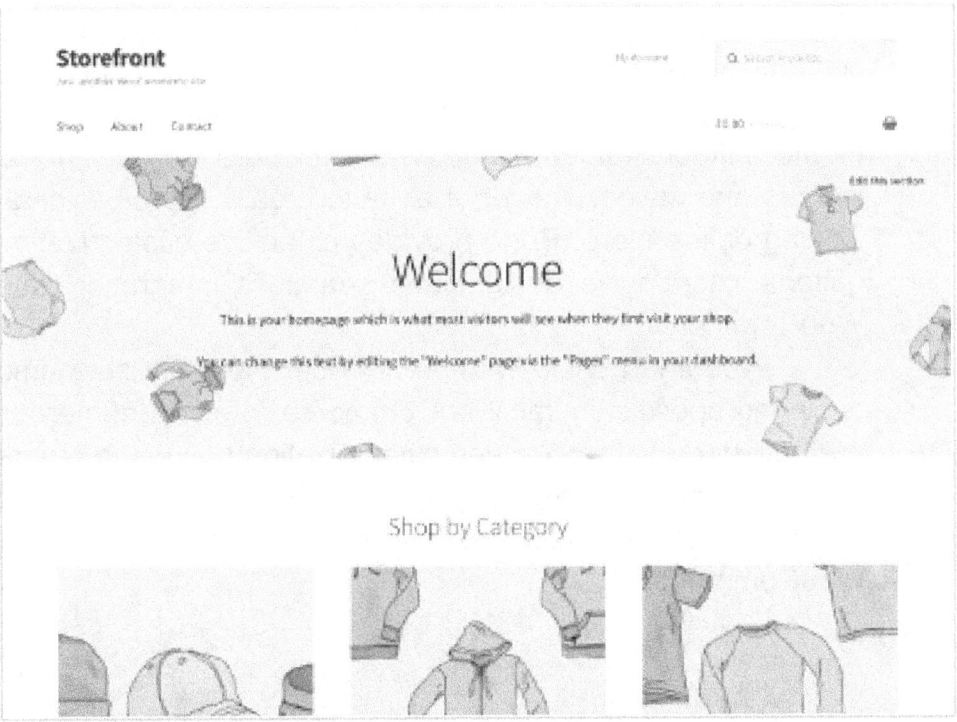

custom layouts. Divi offers numerous pre-designed templates, a user-friendly interface, and full WooCommerce integration. It provides extensive customization options and is suitable for creating various types of online stores.

Astra: Astra is a lightweight and fast-loading theme that is compatible with WooCommerce. It offers a wide range of customizable design options and layouts. Astra also integrates well with popular page builders, making it easy to create unique and visually appealing online stores.

OceanWP: OceanWP is a responsive and feature-rich theme that works well with WooCommerce. It offers a variety of pre-built templates and demos specifically designed for e-commerce. OceanWP provides extensive customization options, fast loading times, and compatibility with popular page builders.

Flatsome: Flatsome is a popular choice for creating beautiful and user-friendly online stores. It offers a range of pre-designed layouts and templates tailored for WooCommerce.

Flatsome comes with a drag-and-drop page builder and customization options to create a unique shopping experience.

Porto: Porto is a highly customizable and feature-rich theme suitable for WooCommerce. It offers multiple demo layouts and styles, making it easy to create a professional-looking online store. Porto provides extensive customization options, responsive design, and seamless integration with WooCommerce.

WoodMart: WoodMart is a modern and stylish theme designed specifically for WooCommerce. It offers numerous pre-built demos, layouts, and customization options to create a unique shopping experience. WoodMart is known for its flexibility, fast loading times, and excellent compatibility with WooCommerce.

_____ NOTE _____

Never try to install a Nulled Theme. A nulled theme refers to a pirated or illegally obtained version of a premium WordPress theme. It is a modified version of a theme that is distributed without the permission or authorization of the original theme developer or author.

Installing a nulled theme, which refers to a pirated or illegally obtained version of a premium theme, is not recommended for several important reasons:

Legal and Ethical Concerns: Nulled themes are distributed without the permission of the original theme developers or authors. By installing and using a nulled theme, you are engaging in copyright infringement, which is illegal and unethical. Supporting the work of theme developers by purchasing their themes ensures that they can continue to create high-quality products and provide ongoing support.

Security Risks: Nulled themes often come bundled with malicious code or backdoors that can compromise the security of your website. Since these themes are obtained from unofficial sources, there is no guarantee of their integrity or safety. The presence of malicious code can lead to various issues, including unauthorized access to your site, data breaches, and potential damage to your reputation.

Lack of Updates and Support: When you purchase a legitimate premium theme, you gain access to regular updates and support from the theme developers. These updates often include bug fixes, security patches, and compatibility improvements with the latest version of WordPress and plugins. Nulled themes, on the other hand, lack official updates and support, leaving your website vulnerable to security vulnerabilities and compatibility issues.

Poor Code Quality and Functionality: Nulled themes are typically modified and distributed by unauthorized sources, resulting in compromised code quality. These themes may contain coding errors, poorly implemented features, and compatibility problems with other plugins or WordPress updates. Using a nulled theme can lead to a subpar website performance, functional limitations, and difficulties in customization.

Reputation and Trust: If your website is built on a nulled theme and it becomes known that you are using illegal or pirated software, it can severely damage your reputation and credibility. Visitors may question the trustworthiness of your website and be hesitant to engage with your content or services.

INSTALLING AND ACTIVATING A THEME

Once you have chosen a WooCommerce-compatible theme, follow these steps to install and activate it:

Access the WordPress Dashboard: Log in to your WordPress admin panel by navigating to yourdomain.com/wp-admin.

Navigate to the Themes Section: In the WordPress dashboard, go to "Appearance" and then click on "Themes."

Add New Theme: Click on the "Add New" button to access the WordPress theme repository. You can search for themes using keywords or browse through the featured, popular, or latest themes.

Upload Theme (If applicable): If you have downloaded a theme from a third-party source or purchased a premium theme, you can upload it by clicking on the "Upload Theme" button and selecting the theme file from your computer.

Install and Activate the Theme: Once you have found

the desired theme, click on the "Install" button to install it. After installation, click on the "Activate" button to activate the theme for your website.

Configure Theme Settings: Depending on the theme, you may have specific customization options available in the WordPress Customizer or a dedicated theme settings panel. Explore these settings to personalize the appearance and functionality of your online store.

Verify WooCommerce Integration: After activating the theme, ensure that WooCommerce is correctly integrated. Go to the WooCommerce settings and review the appearance and layout options to make sure they align with your theme's design.

By following these steps, you can successfully choose and install a WooCommerce-compatible theme for your online store. Remember to regularly update your theme and check for compatibility with new versions of WordPress and WooCommerce to ensure optimal performance and security.

TO INSTALL THE WOOCOMMERCE PLUGIN, FOLLOW THESE STEPS

- Log in to your WordPress website's admin area. You can do this by adding "/wp-admin" at the end of your website's URL (e.g., www.yourwebsite.com/wp-admin).
- Once logged in, navigate to the left-hand sidebar and click on "Plugins."
- Click on the "Add New" button at the top of the page.
- In the search field on the right-hand side, type "WooCommerce" and press Enter.
- The official WooCommerce plugin should appear as the first result. Click on the "Install Now" button next to it.
- WordPress will then download and install the WooCommerce plugin for you. After the installation is complete, you will see an "Activate" button. Click on it to activate the plugin.

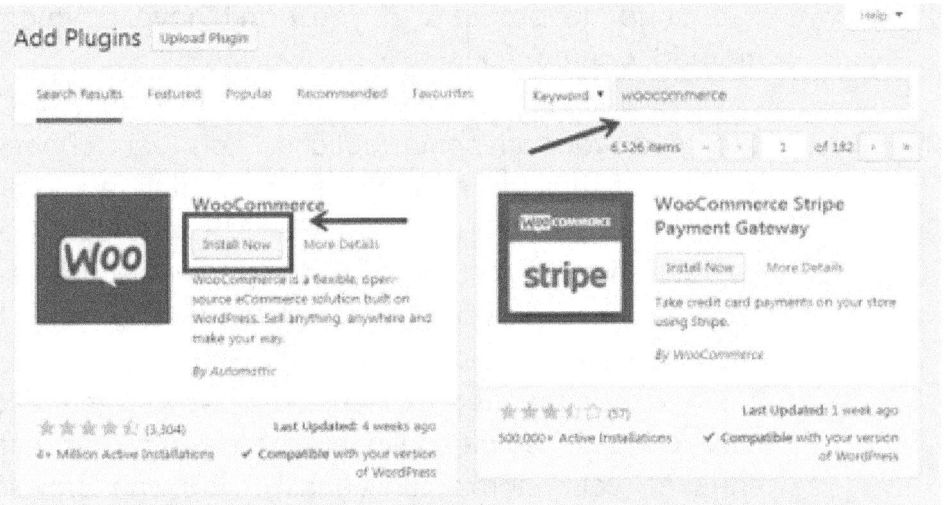

- Once activated, you will be taken to the WooCommerce setup wizard. It will guide you through the initial configuration of your online store. Follow the prompts to set up your store details, payment gateways, shipping options, and more:

Choose Your Store Location: The first step in the Setup Wizard is to select your store's location. Enter your country and address details, as this information will be used for tax calculations and shipping settings. Click on "Continue" to proceed.

Choose Your Industry and Product Types: In this step, you'll be asked to select your industry and the type of products you plan to sell. Choose the options that best describe your business. You can select multiple product types if applicable. Click on "Continue" to move forward.

Choose Your Store's Payment Methods: Next, you'll be prompted to select the payment methods you want to offer to your customers. WooCommerce supports various payment gateways, such as PayPal, Stripe, and offline methods like cash on delivery. Select the payment methods you want to enable and follow the instructions to set them up. Click on

"Continue" to proceed. If you don't have payment method, you can skip.

Configure Shipping Settings: In this step, you'll configure your shipping options. You can choose to enable shipping methods such as flat rate, free shipping, or real-time carriers like UPS or FedEx. Set up your shipping methods according to your business requirements. Click on "Continue" to move forward. If you sell digital products, you can skip.

Recommended Extensions: WooCommerce may suggest some optional extensions that can enhance your store's functionality. You can browse through the recommendations and choose to install any extensions that align with your needs. Click on "Continue" to proceed.

Activate Jetpack (Optional): WooCommerce may ask if you want to activate Jetpack, a powerful plugin that offers additional features and security enhancements. You can choose to activate it or skip this step.

You can also skip the wizard if you prefer to configure everything manually.

- After completing the setup wizard configuration, WooCommerce will be fully installed and ready to use on your WordPress website.

Remember to customize your store's appearance, add products, and configure other settings according to your specific requirements. You can access the WooCommerce settings by clicking on "WooCommerce" in the WordPress admin sidebar.

That's it! You have successfully installed the WooCommerce plugin on your WordPress website. Now you can start building your online store and exploring the various features and options available within WooCommerce.

CUSTOMIZING YOUR WEBSITE'S APPEARANCE

Once you have chosen and installed a WordPress theme for your website, it's time to customize its appearance to align with your brand and create a unique look. In this chapter, we will guide you through the process of customizing the theme's appearance, including adding a logo and customizing the header and footer.

CUSTOMIZING THE THEME'S APPEARANCE

Theme customizing refers to the process of making visual and design changes to a WordPress theme to personalize its appearance and align it with your brand or desired style. Customizing a theme allows you to modify various elements of your website's design, such as colors, typography, layout, header and footer sections, background images, and more. It gives you the flexibility to create

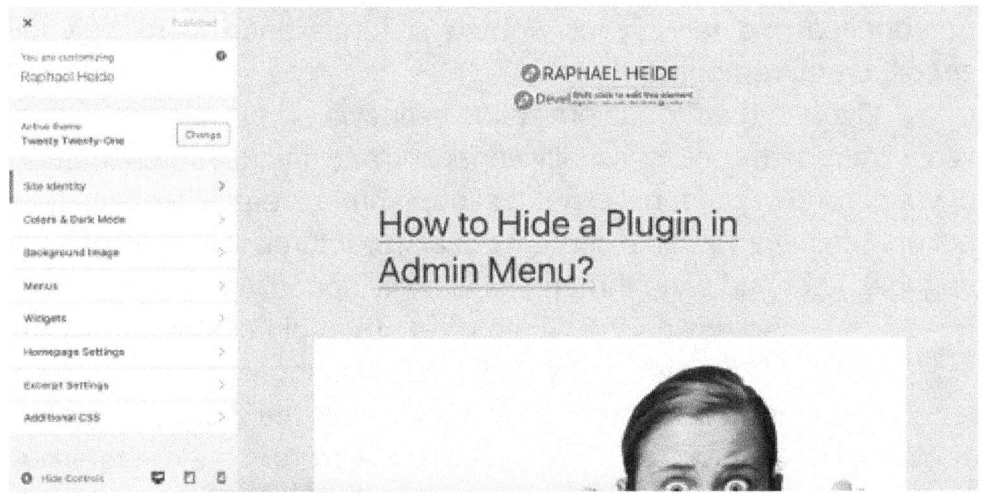

a unique and visually appealing website that reflects your brand identity or personal preferences.

Through the WordPress Customizer, you can access theme customization options and make real-time changes, previewing how they will affect the overall look of your website. This user-friendly interface provides a range of customization settings that can be adjusted without requiring extensive coding knowledge.

Customizing a theme typically involves tasks such as uploading a logo, changing color schemes, selecting fonts, modifying header and footer layouts, adjusting background images, and customizing various other visual elements. The goal is to create a cohesive and visually pleasing website that resonates with your target audience and enhances the user experience.

With theme customization, you have the opportunity to make your website stand out and differentiate it from other sites using the same theme. By incorporating your brand's colors, logo, and unique design elements, you can create a consistent and memorable visual identity for your website.

It's important to note that the customization options available may vary depending on the WordPress theme you have chosen. Some themes offer extensive customization capabilities, providing a wide range of settings and options, while others may have more limited customization features. However, regardless of the theme you select, there are usually ample opportunities to personalize and tailor your website's appearance to meet your specific requirements.

Overall, theme customization empowers you to transform a WordPress theme into a visually appealing and unique representation of your brand or personal style. It allows you to create a website that not only delivers valuable content but also captures the attention and engages your audience through its visually appealing design.

Accessing the Customizer: To begin customizing your theme, navigate to the WordPress dashboard and click on "Appearance" in the sidebar menu. From the dropdown menu, select "Customize." This will open the WordPress Customizer, a powerful tool that allows you to make visual changes to your website.

Site Identity: One of the key aspects of customizing your website's appearance is adding a logo. In the Customizer, look for the "Site Identity" or "Logo" option. Here, you can upload your logo image or choose an existing image from the media library. Adjust the logo size, position, and alignment to ensure it looks visually appealing.

Header Customization: The header section is an important part of your website's appearance. In the Customizer, look for the "Header" or "Header Settings" option. Here, you can customize elements such as the header layout, background color or image, menu placement, and navigation style. Make sure to preview your changes in real-time to ensure they align with your desired design.

Footer Customization: Similar to the header, the footer section can be customized to reflect your brand and add additional functionality. In the Customizer, locate the "Footer" or "Footer Settings" option. Here, you can modify the footer layout, add widgets or content, adjust the color scheme, and display copyright information. Experiment with different configurations to achieve the desired look and feel.

Colors and Typography: Most WordPress themes offer options to customize colors and typography. Look for sections like "Colors," "Typography," or "Fonts" in the Customizer. Here, you can change the colors of various elements such as links, buttons, headings, and backgrounds. Additionally, you can adjust font styles, sizes, and spacing to enhance readability and overall visual appeal.

Background and Images: If you want to set a specific background color or image for your website, explore the "Background" or "Background Image" options in the Customizer. This allows you to choose a solid color, upload an image, or select a predefined pattern to set as the background. Consider using high-quality images that align with your brand's aesthetic.

Additional Customization Options: Depending on the theme you have chosen, there may be additional customization options available in the Customizer. Explore different sections and settings to personalize your website further. This can include options for sidebar layout, blog post styles, social media integration, and more. Take advantage of these features to create a truly unique website.

Remember to save your changes in the Customizer after making any modifications. It's also a good practice to preview your website in different devices and screen sizes to ensure your customizations are responsive and look consistent across all platforms.

By customizing the appearance of your WordPress theme, adding a logo, and customizing the header and footer sections, you can create a visually appealing and branded website that captures the essence of your business or personal brand. Take your time to experiment and find the design elements that resonate with your audience and reflect your unique identity.

CREATE A SHOP PAGE

To create a shopping page in WooCommerce, you'll need to follow these steps:

1 - Create a Shop Page: To display your products on a dedicated shopping page, you need to create a "Shop" page. Go to "Pages" in your admin sidebar and click on "Add New." Give the page a title (e.g., "Shop") and leave the content area blank. Publish the page.

2 - Set the Shop Page in WooCommerce: In your admin sidebar, go to "WooCommerce" and click on "Settings." Then, click on the "Products" tab and go to the "Display" section. Under "Shop Page," select the "Shop" page you created in the previous step from the dropdown menu. Save the changes. Done!

In WordPress, you have the ability to create and manage

menus, giving you control over the navigation structure of your website. To access the menu settings, navigate to the "Appearance" section in your WordPress admin dashboard and select the "Menus" option. Within this menu editor, you can create new menus, configure menu settings, and add various types of menu items, including pages, posts, custom links, or categories. This allows you to customize your website's navigation and ensure a smooth browsing experience for your visitors.

Create New Menu: To create a new menu, click on the "Create a New Menu" button within the "Menus" page. Give your menu a name, select the desired location for the menu, and click the "Create Menu" button. You can then start adding menu items and organizing them within the menu structure.

Menu Settings: In the "Menu Settings" section of the "Menus" page, you can specify the display location for your menus. Depending on your theme, options may include primary menu, secondary menu, footer menu, etc. Select the desired location, save your changes, and the menu will appear in the designated area of your website.

Add Menu Items: To populate your menus with items, you can choose from various content types. Add pages, posts, custom links, or categories to your menu by selecting them from the available options and clicking the "Add to Menu" button. You can then drag and drop the items to rearrange their order within the menu. Add your "Store" page. Save the menu.

ADDING AND MANAGING PRODUCTS IN WOOCOMMERCE

WooCommerce is a powerful plugin that allows you to transform your WordPress website into an e-commerce store. In this chapter, we will explore how to add and manage products in WooCommerce, covering the process of adding simple and variable products and effectively managing inventory and attributes.

First step, you need to give a name and a description for your product:

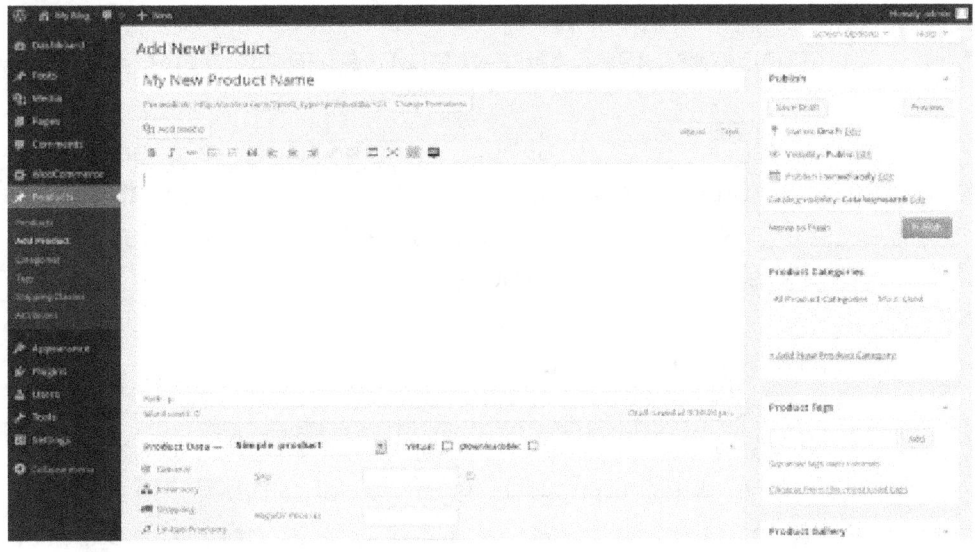

ADDING AN IMAGE OR GALLERY ON YOUR PRODUCT

If you know how to add an image in a post or a page, you will make the same steps: scroll down to the "Product Image" section, which is typically located below the product description.

Click on the "Set product image" or "Set featured image" button.

A media uploader window will appear. You can either upload a new image or select an image from the media library. To upload a new image, click on the "Upload Files" tab and then click on the "Select Files" button. Locate the image file on your computer and click on "Open" to upload it. If you want to use an image from the media library, switch to the "Media Library" tab and select the image you want.

Once the image is uploaded or selected, you will see a thumbnail preview. You can edit the image details, such as the title, alt text, caption, and description, by clicking on the "Edit" link below the thumbnail. It's good practice to provide descriptive alt text for accessibility purposes.

You can add more than one image on products. Just add in Product Gallery.

ADDING SIMPLE AND VARIABLE PRODUCTS

In WooCommerce, a simple product refers to a basic and straightforward product that doesn't have any variations or attributes. It represents a single item that customers can purchase without selecting different options or choices.

1 - Adding Simple Products:

When adding a simple product in WooCommerce, you provide the essential details such as the product name, description, price, SKU (Stock Keeping Unit), and product category. You can also upload product images to showcase the item to potential buyers. However, there are no additional options or variations associated with the product.

Simple products are ideal for items that don't require different options or configurations. For example, if you're selling a t-shirt in a single color and size, you can create a simple product with the product's specific details and set the price accordingly. Customers can add the product to their cart and proceed to checkout without needing to choose different variations.

You can also mark a product as Virtual and/or Downloadable. In the context of e-commerce and specifically WooCommerce, virtual and downloadable products refer to two different types of products that can be sold online:

Virtual Products: Virtual products are intangible goods that are delivered electronically or accessed online. They do not have a physical form or require shipping. Examples of virtual products include software licenses, e-books, online courses, membership subscriptions, or digital music files. When a customer purchases a virtual product, they typically receive access to a download link, login credentials, or a unique license key that enables them to access or download the product.

Downloadable Products: Downloadable products are digital files that customers can download to their devices. These files can be anything from software applications, themes, plugins, images, videos, audio files, documents, or any other type of digital content. When a customer purchases a downloadable product, they are provided with

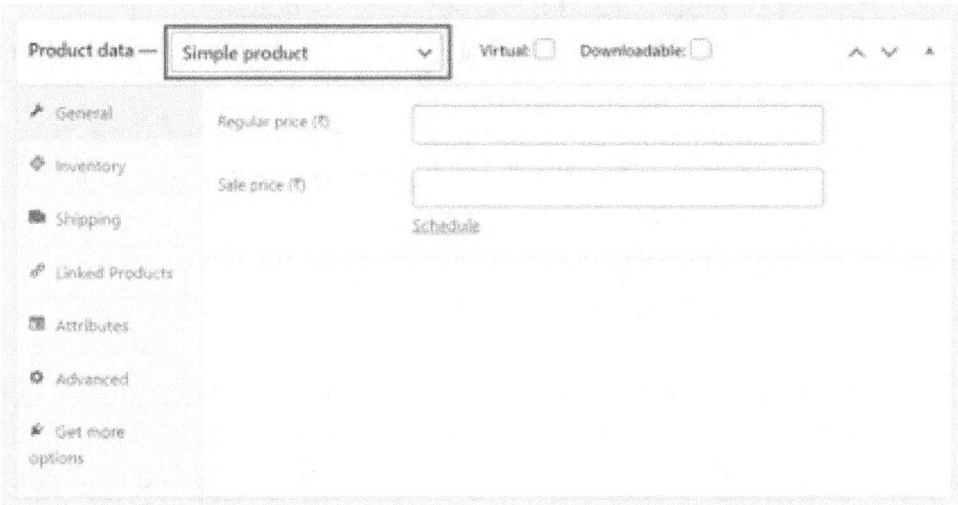

a download link to retrieve the file. The file may be hosted directly on the website or provided through a cloud storage service.

Both virtual and downloadable products offer the convenience of immediate access to the purchased item without the need for physical shipping. They cater to the growing demand for digital goods and online services, providing a seamless buying experience for customers. WooCommerce provides specific settings and features to manage the sale, delivery, and access control of virtual and downloadable products, making it suitable for businesses that sell these types of goods.

How to add a simple product:

- Log in to your WordPress admin dashboard.
- Navigate to the WooCommerce tab and select "Products."
- Click on the "Add Product" button to create a new product.
- Provide the necessary details such as the product name, description, price, SKU (Stock Keeping Unit), and product category.
- Upload product images to showcase the item.
- Set product attributes like color, size, or any other relevant variations.
- Configure shipping options and inventory settings.
- Click on the "Publish" button to make the product live on your website.

2 - Adding Variable Products:

In WooCommerce, a variable product refers to a type of product that has multiple variations or options for customers to choose from. It allows you to offer different variations of a product, such as different sizes, colors, or styles, all within a single product listing.

When creating a variable product in WooCommerce, you define attributes that apply to the product, such as size and color. Each attribute can have multiple options or variations associated with it. For example, if you're selling a t-shirt, you can create attributes for size (small, medium, large) and color (red, blue, green). Each combination of size and color represents a specific variation of the product.

How to add a variable product:

- Follow the initial steps of adding a simple product.
- Enable the "Variable product" option in the product data section.
- Define attributes for the product variations, such as size or color.
- Create different variations by combining attributes and setting unique prices, SKUs, and stock quantities for each.
- Add product images for each variation if necessary.
- Configure additional settings such as shipping and inventory for the variable product.
- Save and publish the product.

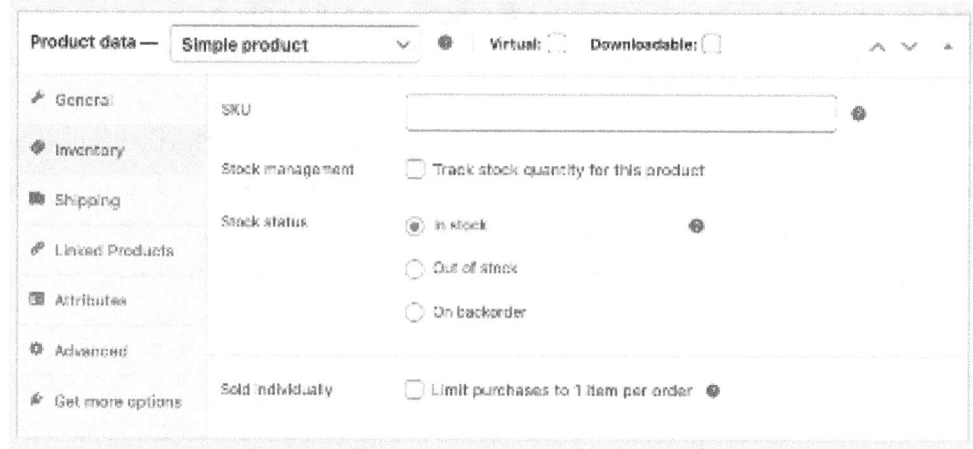

MANAGING PRODUCT INVENTORY AND ATTRIBUTES

1 - Inventory Management:

Inventory management refers to the process of overseeing and controlling the flow of goods or products within a business. In the context of WooCommerce, inventory management involves managing and tracking the stock levels of your products.

Effective inventory management is crucial for an online store as it ensures that you have the right amount of stock available to fulfill customer orders without running out or oversupplying. It involves keeping track of inventory quantities, monitoring product availability, and making informed decisions to optimize stock levels.

- Access the product inventory settings for each product by editing the product in WooCommerce.
- Set the stock status (in stock/out of stock) and manage stock quantities.
- Enable low stock notifications to receive alerts when products are running low.
- Utilize the backorder option if you want to allow customers to purchase items even when they are out of stock.
- Define stock visibility and choose to hide products when they are out of stock.

50

- Save the changes to update the product's inventory settings.

 SKU stands for Stock Keeping Unit. It is a unique identifier assigned to a specific product or item in inventory management. SKUs are used by businesses to track and manage their inventory effectively. The SKU is typically an alphanumeric code or number that provides information about the product, such as its characteristics, attributes, or variations. It helps differentiate between different items in the inventory, including different colors, sizes, models, or versions of a product.

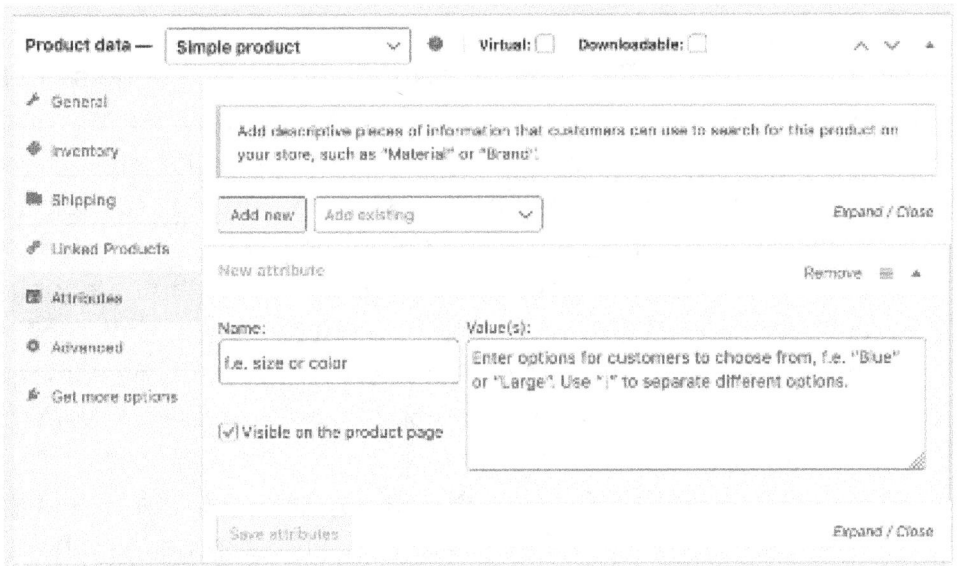

2 - Product Attributes:

Product attributes in WooCommerce are characteristics or properties that define and describe your products. They provide additional information about the product and help customers make informed purchasing decisions. Product attributes can include features like size, color, material, style, or any other relevant attribute that distinguishes one product from another.

Attributes can be classified into two types: global attributes and custom attributes.

Global Attributes: These are attributes that are commonly applicable to multiple products across your store. For example, if you sell clothing, size and color can be global attributes. Global attributes are created once and can be used for multiple products.

Custom Attributes: These are attributes specific to individual products. Custom attributes are created and assigned to a specific product, providing unique information about that product.

Product attributes in WooCommerce allow you to:

Provide Detailed Information: Attributes help you provide detailed specifications about your products, allowing customers to understand their specific characteristics. This information assists customers in making purchase decisions based on their preferences and requirements.

Facilitate Filtering and Searching: Attributes enable customers to filter and search for products based on specific criteria. For example, if you have a clothing store, customers can filter products by size or color, making it easier for them to find the products they are looking for.

Customize Variable Products: Attributes are essential when working with variable products. Variable products have different options or variations, such as different sizes or colors. Attributes are used to define these variations and allow customers to select the specific options they want.

Enhance Product Organization: Attributes help in organizing your product catalog. By assigning attributes to your products, you can group similar products together and create logical categories or product variations.

Managing product attributes in WooCommerce involves creating and assigning attributes to your products. Here's how you can do it:

Creating Global Attributes: In the WooCommerce settings, you can create global attributes that can be used for multiple products. For example, you can create a "Size" attribute with options like Small, Medium, and Large.

Assigning Attributes to Products: Once you have created attributes, you can assign them to individual products. For example, if you have a t-shirt product, you can assign the "Size" attribute with options like Small, Medium, and Large to that product.

Using Attributes in Variable Products: When working with variable products, you can define variations using attributes. For example, for a t-shirt, you can create variations based on different sizes and colors.

By effectively adding and managing products in WooCommerce, you can create a robust and organized e-commerce store. Whether you're offering simple products with fixed attributes or variable products with multiple variations, WooCommerce provides a user-friendly interface to streamline the product management process.

Remember to Save your product.

CONFIGURING PRODUCT CATEGORIES AND ATTRIBUTES

Product categories in WooCommerce allow you to organize and structure your products, making it easier for customers to navigate and find what they are looking for. By creating well-defined categories, you can enhance the browsing experience and improve the overall organization of your online store.

To create product categories in WooCommerce, follow these steps:

- Log in to your WordPress admin dashboard.
- Navigate to WooCommerce > Products > Categories.
- Click on the "Add New Category" button.
- Enter a name for the category and provide a slug (a URL-friendly version of the name).
- Optionally, you can add a description for the category to provide more information to your customers.
- If desired, assign a parent category to create a hierarchical structure.
- Click on the "Add New Category" button to save your changes.

Once you have created product categories, you can assign them to individual products while creating or editing product listings. This helps in organizing your products under relevant categories, ensuring a well-structured catalog.

SETTING UP PRODUCT ATTRIBUTES AND FILTERS

Product attributes and filters play a crucial role in helping customers narrow down their product search and find the specific items they are interested in. WooCommerce provides a flexible system for defining attributes and using them as filters to refine product listings.

Here's how you can set up product attributes and filters in WooCommerce:

- Log in to your WordPress admin dashboard.
- Navigate to WooCommerce > Products > Attributes.
- Click on the "Add New Attribute" button.
- Enter a name for the attribute, such as "Color" or "Size."
- Choose whether the attribute should be used for variations (if you have variable products) and whether it should be visible on the product page.
- Under "Values," add the specific options for the attribute. For example, if the attribute is "Color," you can add options like "Red," "Blue," and "Green."
- Save the attribute.

Once you have set up attributes, you can assign them to individual products or variations:

- When creating or editing a product, navigate to the "Product Data" section.
- Choose the appropriate attribute from the dropdown menu and click "Add."
- Specify the attribute value for that particular product. For example, if the attribute is "Size," you can assign the value "Small" or "Medium" for a t-shirt product.
- Repeat the process for other attributes as needed.

- Save the product.

Using product attributes, you can create filters to allow customers to refine their search based on specific attributes. WooCommerce provides various options for adding attribute filters to your online store, such as using widgets, plugins, or theme features. Consult your theme documentation or consider using plugins specifically designed for product filtering to enhance the search functionality.

By effectively configuring product categories and attributes, you can create a well-organized product catalog and provide customers with an efficient way to find products based on their preferences. Organized categories and attribute filters improve the user experience and make it easier for customers to discover the products they desire.

MANAGING INVENTORY AND STOCK

Efficient inventory management is crucial for any online store, including those powered by WooCommerce. Properly managing your inventory ensures that you can meet customer demand, avoid overselling, and maintain accurate stock information. Here are some best practices for managing your inventory effectively:

Regular Inventory Audits: Conduct regular audits to reconcile your physical inventory with the stock records in your WooCommerce store. This helps identify any discrepancies and ensures accurate stock levels.

Set Reorder Points: Determine the minimum quantity of a product at which you need to reorder to avoid stockouts. Set up reorder points to receive alerts when stock levels reach a specific threshold.

Track Product Performance: Monitor the performance of your products to identify fast-selling items and slow-moving inventory. This information can guide your purchasing decisions and help optimize your product assortment.

Centralize Inventory Management: If you sell products across multiple channels (e.g., online store, physical store, marketplaces), consider using centralized inventory management tools or integrations to synchronize stock levels and prevent overselling.

Streamline Supplier Relationships: Maintain strong relationships with your suppliers to ensure timely deliveries and better control over your inventory. Communicate regularly and establish efficient processes for ordering, receiving, and managing supplier inventory.

Utilize Barcode Scanning: Implement barcode scanning systems to expedite inventory management tasks, such as receiving new stock or performing stocktakes. Barcode scanning minimizes human error and improves efficiency.

Consider Dropshipping: If managing inventory and stock becomes challenging, explore dropshipping options. With dropshipping, the supplier directly fulfills customer orders, eliminating the need for you to stock and ship products.

UTILIZING STOCK STATUS AND BACKORDERS

WooCommerce provides built-in features to help you manage stock status and handle backorders. These features enable you to maintain accurate stock information and allow customers to place orders even when products are temporarily out of stock.

Stock Status: Each product in WooCommerce can have a stock status, indicating whether it is in stock or out of stock. When a product's stock reaches zero, the stock status can automatically update to "Out of Stock," preventing customers from placing orders. You can customize stock status messages to inform customers about stock availability.

Backorders: Backorders allow customers to place orders for products that are out of stock. When enabled, customers can still purchase products even if the stock level is zero. You can configure backorders to be allowed, not allowed, or only allowed for specific products. Managing backorders requires careful monitoring to ensure prompt fulfillment once the stock is replenished.

To manage stock status and backorders in WooCommerce:

- Log in to your WordPress admin dashboard.

- Navigate to WooCommerce > Settings > Products > Inventory.

- Configure the options under the "Stock Options" section, such as enabling stock management, setting stock display format, and managing backorders.

- Save your changes.

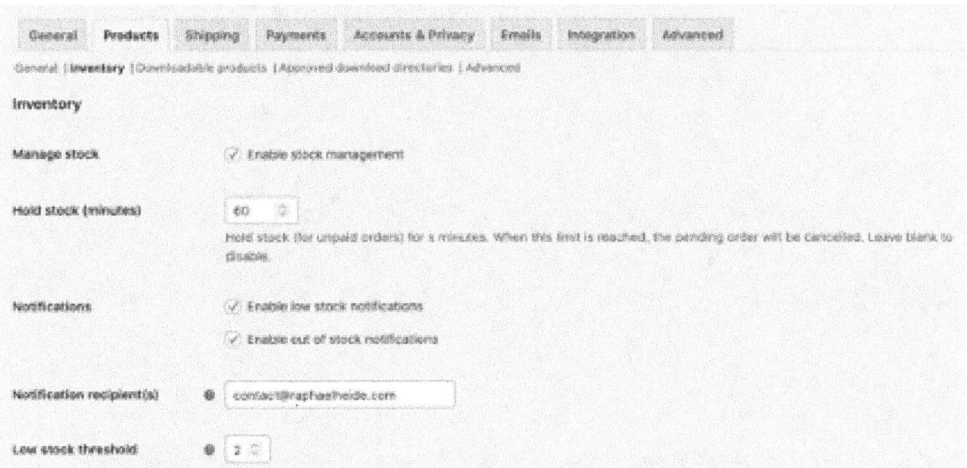

By utilizing stock status and backorders effectively, you can provide customers with accurate stock information and the flexibility to place orders even when products are temporarily unavailable. This helps you maintain customer satisfaction and optimize sales while ensuring efficient stock management practices.

SETTING UP PAYMENT GATEWAYS

Setting up Payment Gateways is a critical step in creating a seamless and secure online shopping experience for your customers. WooCommerce offers a variety of payment gateway options that you can integrate with your store. In this chapter, we will guide you through the process of configuring popular payment gateways such as PayPal, Stripe, and ensuring secure payment processing.

CONFIGURING PAYPAL, STRIPE, AND OTHER PAYMENT GATEWAYS

WooCommerce provides built-in support for several payment gateways, including PayPal and Stripe. We have different payment gateways. The payment gateways are listed in 4 types:

Form based: This is where the user must click a button on a form that then redirects them to the payment processor on the gateway's own website. Example: PayPal standard, Authorize.net DPM.

iFrame based: This is when the gateway payment system is loaded inside an iframe on your store. Example: SagePay Form, PayPal Advanced.

Direct: This is when the payment fields are shown directly on the checkout page and the payment is made when 'place order' is pressed. Example: PayPal Pro, Authorize.net .

Offline: No online payment is made. Example: Cheque, Bank Transfer

For online payment you need to install the gateway plugin: PayPal, Stripe or other. To install, go in plugin and search the payment gateway. Active the plugin.

HOW DOES A PAYMENT GATEWAY WORK?

You need to have an account in a gateway payment, like PayPal or Stripe.

Remember: there are certain restrictions and limitations on what you can sell based on legal, ethical, and platform-specific guidelines. Here are a few examples of items that may be restricted or prohibited on WooCommerce AND Payment Gateways:

- Illegal or Prohibited Products: It is important to comply with local laws and regulations. You cannot sell products or services that are illegal, such as drugs, firearms, counterfeit goods, or stolen items. Additionally, certain regulated products, such as prescription drugs or restricted chemicals, may require specific licenses or permits to be sold.

- Restricted or Adult Content: WooCommerce has guidelines regarding adult-oriented materials, explicit content, or products that are considered offensive or inappropriate. Selling explicit content or products intended for adult use may violate platform policies.

- Copyrighted or Trademarked Products: Selling counterfeit or unauthorized copyrighted or trademarked goods is strictly prohibited. Ensure that you have the necessary rights or permissions to sell branded products to avoid legal issues.

- Services or Digital Products without Appropriate Licenses: If you are selling services or digital products, ensure that you have the appropriate licenses or permissions to distribute them. This includes software, themes, plugins, music, videos, or e-books. Violating intellectual property rights may lead to legal consequences.

- Hazardous Materials: WooCommerce may have restrictions on selling hazardous materials, such as chemicals, explosives, or substances that pose a safety risk.

- Live Animals or Endangered Species: Selling live animals or products made from endangered species is typically prohibited due to ethical and legal concerns.

TO SET UP A PAYPAL ACCOUNT TO SELL ON WOOCOMMERCE

- Visit the PayPal website: Go to www.paypal.com and click on the "Sign Up" button.

- Choose an account type: Select the appropriate account type for your business. PayPal offers both personal and business accounts. For selling on WooCommerce, it's recommended to create a business account.

- Provide your email address: Enter your email address, which will be associated with your PayPal account. Make sure to use an email address that you have access to and can monitor regularly.

- Create a password: Choose a secure password for your PayPal account. It should be a combination of letters, numbers, and special characters to ensure the account's safety.

- Fill in the required information: PayPal will ask for your business information, including your business name, address, phone number, and website (your WooCommerce store). Provide accurate details to complete the setup process.

- Set up payment preferences: On the next page, you'll have the option to choose your preferred payment methods. Select the relevant options for your business. PayPal offers various options, including accepting payments through credit or debit cards, bank transfers, and PayPal account balances.

- Link your bank account or credit/debit card: To receive payments from your WooCommerce store, you need to link your PayPal account to your bank account or credit/debit card. Follow the instructions provided by PayPal to complete this step. PayPal will guide you through the verification process to ensure secure transactions.

- Verify your PayPal account: PayPal may require you to verify your account by confirming your email address and providing additional information, such as your bank account details. Follow the instructions provided by PayPal to complete the verification process.

- Enable PayPal as a payment gateway in WooCommerce: Once your PayPal account is set up and verified, you can integrate it with your WooCommerce store. In your WordPress admin area, go to "WooCommerce" > "Settings" > "Payments." Click on the "Set up" button for PayPal, and follow the instructions to connect your PayPal account.

- Configure PayPal settings in WooCommerce: Within the WooCommerce settings, you can configure various options related to PayPal, such as enabling PayPal Standard, PayPal Express Checkout, or PayPal Payments Pro. Choose the appropriate options based on your preferences and business needs.

- Test your payment setup: It's important to perform a test transaction to ensure that your PayPal integration is working correctly. Make a small purchase on your own

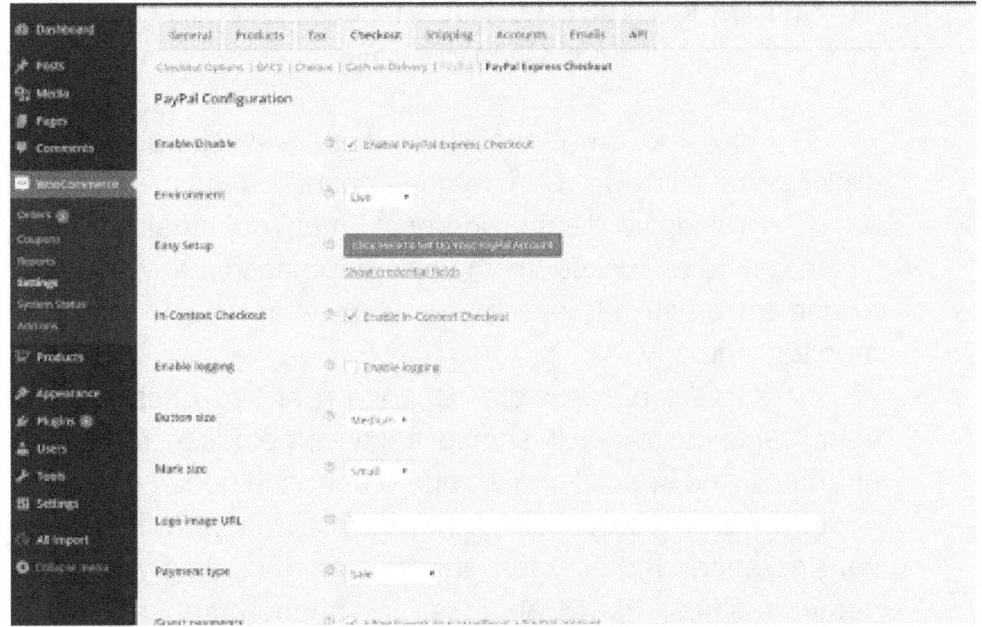

WooCommerce store using a different PayPal account or a test mode provided by PayPal. This allows you to verify that payments are processed successfully and that the funds are being deposited into your account. In Environment, you can check "Sandbox" to test if your gateway payment is working. You can use any credit card number to test and you can see in PayPal website if is working. When "Live" is checked, means your website will receive real payment.

- Once you've completed these steps, your PayPal account will be set up to accept payments on your WooCommerce store. Customers will be able to choose PayPal as a payment method during the checkout process, and their payments will be securely processed through PayPal's payment gateway.

Remember to regularly monitor your PayPal account for incoming payments and manage any necessary settings or disputes through the PayPal dashboard.

TO SET UP A STRIPE ACCOUNT FOR SELLING ON WOOCOMMERCE

- Visit the Stripe website: Go to www.stripe.com and click on the "Sign Up" or "Create Account" button.

- Provide your email address: Enter your email address, which will be associated with your Stripe account. Make sure to use an email address that you have access to and can monitor regularly.

- Create a password: Choose a strong password for your Stripe account. It should be a combination of letters, numbers, and special characters to enhance security.

- Fill in the required information: Stripe will ask for your personal and business information, including your legal name, business name, address, and phone number. Provide accurate details to complete the setup process.

- Verify your email address: Stripe will send you an email with a verification link. Click on the link to verify your email address and activate your Stripe account.

- Provide additional business information: Stripe may require additional details about your business, such as your website URL (your WooCommerce store), industry type, and business structure. Fill in the required information accurately.

- Set up payment preferences: On the next page, you'll have the option to choose your preferred payment methods. Select the relevant options for your business. Stripe offers various options, including credit and debit cards, digital wallets, and more.

- Set up payout preferences: Stripe allows you to configure how you want to receive funds from your sales. Choose your desired payout frequency (daily, weekly, or monthly) and provide the necessary bank account details for receiving payouts.

- Enable Stripe as a payment gateway in WooCommerce: Once your Stripe account is set up, you can integrate it with your WooCommerce store. In your WordPress admin area, go to "WooCommerce" > "Settings" > "Payments." Click on the "Set up" button for Stripe, and follow the instructions to connect your Stripe account.

- Configure Stripe settings in WooCommerce: Within the WooCommerce settings, you can configure various options related to Stripe, such as enabling Stripe payments, enabling Stripe Checkout, and managing currencies and other settings. Choose the appropriate options based on your preferences and business needs.

- Test your payment setup: It's important to perform a test transaction to ensure that your Stripe integration is working correctly. Make a small purchase on your own WooCommerce store using a test credit card number provided by Stripe. This allows you to verify that payments are processed successfully and that the funds are being deposited into your Stripe account.

- Once you've completed these steps, your Stripe account will be set up to accept payments on your WooCommerce store. Customers will be able to choose Stripe as a payment method during the checkout process, and their payments will be securely processed through Stripe's payment gateway.

Remember to regularly monitor your Stripe account for incoming payments and manage any necessary settings or disputes through the Stripe dashboard.

ANOTHER PAYMENT GATEWAYS

The process looks like PayPal or Stripe. You need to create your account in the gateway and continue the setup in your WooCommerce:

- Navigate to WooCommerce > Settings > Payments.
- Enable the payment gateway you want to configure, such as PayPal or Stripe.

- Enter the required credentials and information for the selected payment gateway. This may include API keys, account details, or email addresses associated with your payment gateway account.

- Configure additional settings specific to the payment gateway, such as enabling sandbox mode for testing purposes, setting up currency options, or customizing payment confirmation messages.

- Save your changes.

Ensure that you thoroughly test the payment gateway integration to ensure it is functioning correctly before accepting live payments.

It's worth noting that there are many other payment gateway options available for WooCommerce, including Authorize.Net, Square, and Amazon Pay, among others. Each payment gateway may have slightly different configuration requirements. Refer to the respective documentation or support resources provided by the payment gateway provider for detailed instructions on configuring them.

Below you can see the payment gateway fee. Remember, the gateway can change the change in any time. It's better check the gateway website.

Payment Gateway	Transaction Fee
Stripe	2.9% + 0.30 per transaction
PayPal Pro	2.9% + 0.30 per transaction
Square	2.65% + $0.30 per transaction
Authorize.net	2.9% + 0.30 per transaction
Amazon Pay	2.9% + 0.30 per transaction

ENSURING SECURE PAYMENT PROCESSING

When setting up payment gateways, it is crucial to prioritize the security of your customers' payment information. The gateway payment companies use the best secure payment processing. Here are some essential measures to ensure secure payment processing:

SSL Certificate: Obtain an SSL (Secure Sockets Layer) certificate for your website. SSL encrypts the data transmitted between your customers' browsers and your website, protecting sensitive information like credit card details. Many hosting providers offer free or affordable SSL certificates.

PCI Compliance: Familiarize yourself with the Payment Card Industry Data Security Standard (PCI DSS) requirements. Ensure that your website and payment gateway integration adhere to these standards to protect cardholder data and maintain a secure environment.

Payment Tokenization: Utilize payment tokenization, a method that replaces sensitive card data with a unique token. Tokenization helps ensure that sensitive payment information is not stored on your servers, reducing the risk of data breaches.

Two-Factor Authentication: Implement two-factor authentication for your WooCommerce admin dashboard and payment gateway accounts. This adds an extra layer of security by requiring a second form of verification, such as a unique code sent to a mobile device, in addition to the password.

Regular Updates and Security Monitoring: Keep your WooCommerce, payment gateway plugins, and other website components up to date with the latest security patches. Monitor your website for any potential vulnerabilities and promptly address any security issues.

By following these security practices, you can create a safe environment for processing customer payments and build trust with your audience.

It's important to note that each payment gateway has its own security features and recommendations. Familiarize yourself with the specific security measures suggested by your chosen payment gateway provider and implement them accordingly to ensure the highest level of payment security for your customers.

CONFIGURING SHIPPING OPTIONS

Setting up shipping options is a crucial aspect of managing an e-commerce store. WooCommerce provides robust tools to help you configure various shipping zones, methods, and calculate accurate shipping costs. In this chapter, we will guide you through the process of configuring shipping options in WooCommerce.

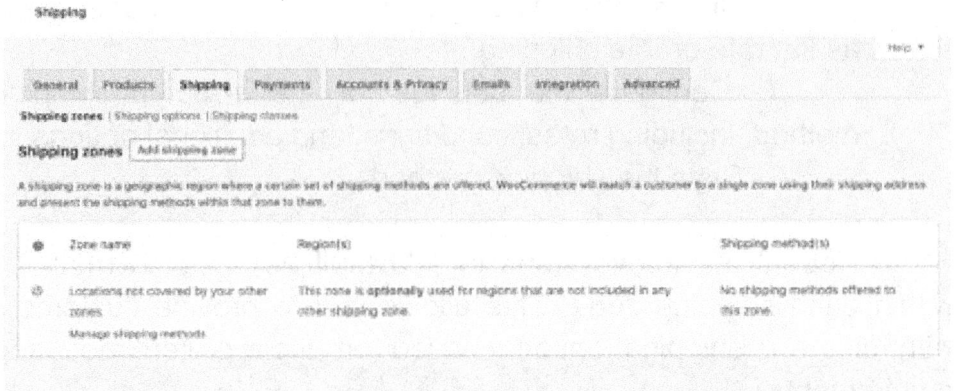

SETTING UP SHIPPING ZONES AND METHODS

WooCommerce allows you to define shipping zones based on geographical regions where you will provide shipping services. Here's how you can set up shipping zones and methods:

- Log in to your WordPress admin dashboard.
- Navigate to WooCommerce > Settings > Shipping.
- Click on the "Shipping Zones" tab.
- Add a new shipping zone by clicking on the "Add

shipping zone" button.

 - Enter a name for the shipping zone, such as "Domestic" or "International."

 - Specify the regions or countries included in the shipping zone. You can choose specific countries, regions within a country, or even exclude certain locations.

 - Save the shipping zone.

Once you have set up shipping zones, you can configure shipping methods within each zone. WooCommerce offers various shipping methods, including flat rate, free shipping, local pickup, and more. Here's how you can configure shipping methods:

 - Click on the desired shipping zone.

 - Click on the "Add shipping method" button.

 - Choose the shipping method you want to offer, such as flat rate or free shipping.

 - Configure the settings for the selected shipping method, including rates, conditions, and additional options.

 - Save the shipping method.

Repeat the above steps to add multiple shipping methods within each shipping zone. This allows you to provide customers with different shipping options based on their preferences and requirements.

CALCULATING SHIPPING COSTS

Accurately calculating shipping costs is crucial to ensure transparency and prevent unexpected expenses for both you and your customers. WooCommerce provides several options for calculating shipping costs based on various factors such as weight, dimensions, destination, and more. Here's how you can set up shipping cost calculations:

- Click on the desired shipping method within a shipping zone.

- Configure the shipping cost settings based on your preferred calculation method.

Flat Rate: Set a fixed shipping cost for all products or specific categories.

Weight-Based: Set shipping costs based on the total weight of the order.

Price-Based: Set shipping costs based on the order's total value.

Dimensional Weight: Calculate shipping costs based on the package's dimensions and weight.

Real-Time Rates: Enable integration with shipping carriers to fetch real-time rates based on the products' details and destination.

Table Rate: Create custom shipping cost tables based on various conditions like weight, price, quantity, and destination.

- Set up the specific rates or conditions for the selected calculation method.

- Save the shipping method.

It's important to regularly review and update your shipping options and cost calculations to ensure they align with your business requirements and any changes in shipping carrier rates or regulations.

By configuring shipping zones, methods, and accurate cost calculations, you can provide a seamless and reliable shipping experience for your customers.

MANAGING ORDERS AND CUSTOMER DATA

Once your e-commerce store is up and running, efficiently managing orders and customer data is crucial for providing excellent customer service. WooCommerce offers powerful tools to process orders, fulfill them promptly, and keep track of customer information. In this chapter, we will guide you through the process of managing orders and customer data effectively.

PROCESSING AND FULFILLING ORDERS

Processing and fulfilling orders refers to the steps involved in managing customer orders and ensuring that they are successfully delivered to the customers. It is an essential aspect of running an e-commerce store and involves various tasks to streamline the order fulfillment process.

Order Management Dashboard: WooCommerce provides an intuitive order management dashboard where you can view, process, and fulfill orders. To access it, log in to your WordPress admin dashboard and navigate to WooCommerce > Orders.

Order Statuses: WooCommerce allows you to assign different statuses to orders, such as "Pending Payment," "Processing," "Completed," "On Hold," or "Cancelled." This helps you keep track of each order's progress and take appropriate actions.

Order Processing Workflow: Once an order is placed,

you can process it by taking the following steps:
- Review the order details, including products, quantities, and customer information.
- Verify payment status and confirm if payment has been received.
- Prepare the order for shipment or fulfillment.
- Update the order status to reflect the current stage of processing.
- Generate and print shipping labels, invoices, or packing slips if necessary.
- Fulfill the order by packaging the products and arranging for shipping or pickup.

PAYMENT STATUS

In WooCommerce, the payment status refers to the state of a customer's payment for an order. It helps track and manage the payment process. Here are the common payment statuses in WooCommerce:

Pending: The payment is yet to be processed or confirmed. It often indicates that the customer has initiated the payment but it is awaiting completion, such as with offline payment methods like bank transfers or checks.

On Hold: The payment has been received, but there may be some additional verification or manual review required before the order can be fulfilled. This status is commonly used for orders that may have triggered fraud alerts or when further action is needed.

Processing: The payment has been successfully received, and the order is being processed for fulfillment. This status indicates that the payment has been authorized and is in progress. The order is typically being prepared for shipment or delivery.

Completed: The payment for the order has been

successfully processed, and the order has been fulfilled. This status indicates that the payment has been received in full, and the goods or services have been delivered or made available to the customer.

Refunded: The payment for the order has been refunded to the customer, either partially or in full. This status is used when a refund has been issued for a specific order.

Failed: The payment attempt has failed, and the customer's payment was not successful. This status indicates that the payment process was not completed, and the order may be canceled or pending further action.

The colors associated with these payment statuses may vary depending on the WooCommerce theme you are using or any customizations you have made. However, the default colors used in WooCommerce are:

Pending: Yellow or orange.
On Hold: Orange or light blue.
Processing: Blue or light green.
Completed: Green.
Refunded: Light gray.
Failed: Red.

Date	Status	Total
7 mins ago	Completed	$52.00
7 mins ago	Pending payment	$47.00
7 mins ago	Completed	$61.00
8 mins ago	Failed	$27.00
8 mins ago	On hold	$89.00
8 mins ago	Processing	$42.00
8 mins ago	Processing	$157.00
8 mins ago	Cancelled	$20.00
8 mins ago	Refunded	$79.00 $0.00

These colors provide a visual representation of the payment status, making it easier to identify the status of orders at a glance in the WooCommerce admin dashboard or order overview.

MANAGING CUSTOMER INFORMATION AND ORDERS

Managing customer information and orders involves efficiently organizing and maintaining data related to your customers and their orders. It is crucial for providing excellent customer service, order tracking, and building long-term customer relationships.

Customer Profiles: WooCommerce stores detailed customer information, including billing and shipping addresses, email addresses, and order history. You can access customer profiles by clicking on their name within an order or by navigating to WooCommerce > Customers.

Order Details and Notes: Each order in WooCommerce contains relevant details, such as order number, date, items purchased, and transaction information. You can also add notes to orders to document specific interactions or requirements related to the order.

Customer Communication: WooCommerce allows you to communicate with customers directly through the platform. You can send order-related emails, update customers on the status of their orders, or address any queries or concerns they may have.

Order Actions: WooCommerce provides various actions you can perform on orders, such as:

- Updating order status: Change the status of an order based on its progress.

- Refunding orders: Process refunds for canceled or returned items.

- Resending order notifications: Send email notifications to customers regarding their orders.

- Adding order notes: Record important information

or instructions related to the order.
- Printing invoices or shipping labels: Generate and print necessary documentation for order fulfillment.

Regularly reviewing and managing customer data and orders helps you provide personalized service, address any issues promptly, and ensure a smooth shopping experience for your customers.

ENHANCING YOUR WOOCOMMERCE STORE WITH PLUGINS

Plugins play a crucial role in extending the functionality of your WooCommerce store and adding new features to enhance the overall shopping experience. In this chapter, we will explore the essential plugins for WooCommerce and guide you through the process of installing and configuring plugin extensions.

ESSENTIAL PLUGINS FOR WOOCOMMERCE

Payment Gateway Plugins: WooCommerce offers several payment gateway options by default, but depending on your business needs, you may require additional payment methods. Install and configure payment gateway plugins like PayPal, Stripe, or Authorize. net to offer customers a wide range of secure payment options.

SEO Plugins: Enhance the visibility of your WooCommerce store in search engine results by utilizing SEO plugins. These plugins help optimize your product pages, meta tags, and URLs for better search engine rankings. Popular SEO plugins include Yoast SEO and All in One SEO Pack.

Analytics and Reporting Plugins: Gain valuable insights into your store's performance, customer behavior, and sales trends with analytics and reporting plugins. These plugins provide comprehensive reports, statistics, and tracking tools to help you make data-driven decisions. Consider installing plugins like Google Analytics for WooCommerce or MonsterInsights.

Marketing and Promotions Plugins: Boost your marketing efforts and increase sales by leveraging marketing and promotions plugins. These plugins offer features like cart abandonment recovery, discounts, coupons, email marketing integration, and social media integration. Consider plugins like Mailchimp for WooCommerce or YITH WooCommerce Coupon.

Product Reviews Plugins: Encourage customer feedback and build trust by integrating product reviews plugins. These plugins allow customers to leave reviews and ratings for products, which can greatly influence the purchasing decisions of potential customers. Consider plugins like WooCommerce Product Reviews Pro or YITH WooCommerce Advanced Reviews.

Security Plugins: Protect your WooCommerce store from security threats and ensure the safety of customer data by installing security plugins. These plugins help prevent hacking attempts, malware infections, and unauthorized access. Popular security plugins for WooCommerce include Sucuri, Wordfence, or iThemes Security.

INSTALLING AND CONFIGURING PLUGIN EXTENSIONS

Before installing any plugin, research its reputation, compatibility with your version of WooCommerce, user reviews, and support documentation. Choose reliable plugins from reputable sources such as the official WordPress plugin repository or well-known plugin developers.

Install Plugins: From your WordPress dashboard, navigate to "Plugins" and click on "Add New." Search for the desired plugin by name or browse through the featured and popular plugins. Click "Install Now" next to the plugin you want to install.

Activate Plugins: After installation, click on "Activate" to enable the plugin on your WooCommerce store. Once activated, you may need to go through a setup process or configure the plugin's settings according to your preferences.

Update Plugins Regularly: Keep your plugins up to date by regularly checking for updates. Plugin updates often include bug fixes, security patches, and new features. Updates can be performed from the "Plugins" page or through automatic updates enabled for specific plugins.

Configure Plugin Settings: Each plugin will have its own settings and configuration options. Take the time to explore and configure the plugin according to your specific requirements. Refer to the plugin's documentation or support resources for guidance on how to set it up properly.

Remember to choose plugins that align with your business needs, consider their compatibility with your WooCommerce version, and regularly update them to ensure optimal performance and security for your store.

By leveraging essential plugins for WooCommerce and carefully configuring their settings, you can enhance your store's functionality, streamline processes, and provide an exceptional shopping experience for your customers.

OPTIMIZING YOUR WEBSITE FOR SEARCH ENGINES (SEO)

In today's digital landscape, search engine optimization (SEO) is crucial for driving organic traffic to your WooCommerce website and improving its visibility in search engine results. In this chapter, we will explore the implementation of SEO best practices and guide you through the process of optimizing product pages and metadata for better search engine rankings.

IMPLEMENTING SEO BEST PRACTICES

SEO (Search Engine Optimization) best practices refer to a set of techniques and strategies that are widely recognized and recommended for improving the visibility and rankings of a website in search engine results pages. These practices aim to optimize various aspects of a website to make it more search engine-friendly, ultimately attracting organic traffic and increasing its chances of being discovered by potential customers.

Keyword Research: Conduct thorough keyword research to identify the relevant keywords and phrases that potential customers are using to search for products similar to yours. Use keyword research tools like Google Keyword Planner, SEMrush, or Ahrefs to discover high-volume and low-competition keywords that align with your business.

On-Page Optimization: Optimize your product pages by incorporating relevant keywords in the page titles, headings, URLs, and content. Ensure that your content is unique, descriptive, and provides value to the users. Optimize image alt tags, meta descriptions, and meta tags to improve search engine visibility.

User-Friendly URLs: Create user-friendly and keyword-rich URLs for your product pages. Avoid long, confusing URLs with irrelevant strings of numbers or symbols. Use descriptive words that accurately represent the content of the page.

Mobile Responsiveness: Ensure that your WooCommerce website is mobile-friendly and responsive. With the increasing use of mobile devices for online shopping, search engines prioritize mobile-friendly websites in their rankings. Optimize your website's design, layout, and functionality for seamless mobile browsing.

Site Speed Optimization: Improve your website's loading speed to enhance user experience and search engine rankings. Compress images, minimize CSS and JavaScript files, utilize caching plugins, and choose a reliable web hosting provider to optimize site speed.

OPTIMIZING PRODUCT PAGES AND METADATA

Optimizing product pages and metadata is a crucial aspect of SEO that focuses on improving the visibility and relevance of your individual product pages in search engine results.

Product Descriptions: Craft unique and compelling product descriptions that are informative, engaging, and include relevant keywords. Focus on highlighting the benefits, features, and unique selling points of your products. Avoid duplicate content and provide valuable information that helps customers make informed purchase decisions.

Meta Titles and Descriptions: **Customize meta titles and** descriptions for each product page. Meta titles should be concise, keyword-rich, and accurately represent the product.

Meta descriptions should provide a compelling summary that entices users to click on your listing in search engine results.

Image Optimization: Optimize product images by using descriptive file names and alt tags that include relevant keywords. Compress images without compromising quality to improve page load times. High-quality, visually appealing images can also improve user engagement and conversions.

Structured Data Markup: Implement structured data markup, such as Schema.org, to provide search engines with additional information about your products. This helps search engines understand the context and attributes of your products, potentially leading to enhanced search engine results, such as rich snippets.

Internal Linking: Implement internal linking strategies to improve navigation and crawlability within your website. Link relevant product pages together using descriptive anchor text. This helps search engines discover and index your pages more effectively while also improving user experience by providing easy access to related products.

Regularly monitor your website's performance in search engine rankings using tools like Google Search Console or third-party SEO plugins. Analyze key metrics such as organic traffic, keyword rankings, and click-through rates to identify areas for improvement and refine your SEO strategy accordingly.

By implementing SEO best practices, optimizing product pages, and leveraging metadata effectively, you can improve your WooCommerce website's visibility, attract organic traffic, and drive more conversions and sales.

IMPLEMENTING ANALYTICS AND TRACKING

Analytics and tracking are essential for gaining insights into the performance of your WooCommerce store and understanding user behavior. In this chapter, we will explore the importance of analytics and guide you through the process of setting up Google Analytics and tracking conversions and performance metrics.

SETTING UP GOOGLE ANALYTICS

Google Analytics is a powerful tool that provides valuable data about your website's traffic, user behavior, and conversions. Here's how you can set up Google Analytics for your WooCommerce store:

Create a Google Analytics Account: Visit the Google Analytics website and sign in with your Google account or create a new one if you don't have an account already.

Set Up a Property: Once you're logged in, click on the "Admin" tab, and under the "Account" column, click on "Create Account." Fill in the required information, such as the account name and website URL, and click "Next."

Configure Tracking Settings: On the next screen, select "Web" as the type of property you want to track. Enter the website name, URL, and industry category. Adjust any additional settings according to your preferences and click "Create."

Get Tracking ID: After creating the property, you'll

be provided with a Tracking ID. Copy the code snippet that starts with "UA-" as you'll need it for the next step.

Install Tracking Code: In your WordPress admin dashboard, go to "Appearance" and select "Theme Editor." Find the "header.php" file and paste the Google Analytics tracking code just before the closing </head> tag. Save the changes.

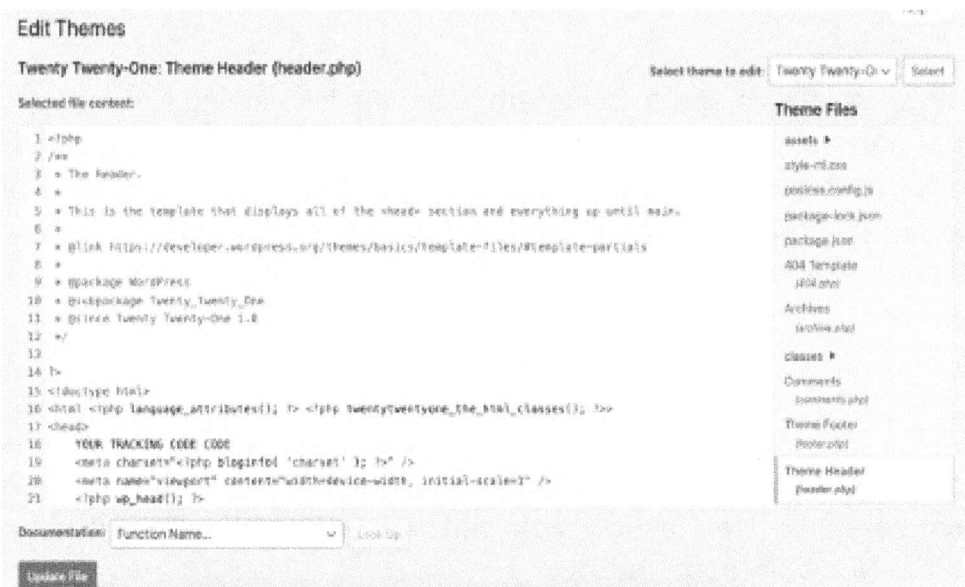

Verify Installation: To ensure that the tracking code is installed correctly, visit your website and navigate to a few pages. Then, go back to your Google Analytics account, click on the "Reporting" tab, and check if real-time data is being tracked.

TRACKING CONVERSIONS AND PERFORMANCE METRICS

Tracking conversions and performance metrics is crucial for understanding the effectiveness of your marketing efforts and optimizing your WooCommerce store. Here are some key metrics to track:

Conversion Tracking: Set up conversion tracking in Google Analytics to monitor important actions on your website, such as completed purchases, newsletter sign-ups, or contact form submissions. You can create goals and track their completion, allowing you to measure the success of your marketing campaigns.

Revenue and Sales Metrics: Monitor revenue and sales metrics to evaluate the financial performance of your WooCommerce store. Track metrics such as total revenue, average order value, conversion rate, and top-selling products. These insights can help you make informed decisions to improve sales and profitability.

Traffic Sources: Analyze the sources of traffic to your website, including organic search, paid advertising, social media, and referrals. This information helps you understand which channels are driving the most traffic and conversions, enabling you to allocate your marketing resources effectively.

User Behavior: Gain insights into user behavior by analyzing metrics such as page views, time on site, bounce rate, and exit pages. Understand how users navigate through your website, identify areas of improvement, and optimize the user experience to encourage engagement and conversions.

E-commerce Tracking: Enable e-commerce tracking in Google Analytics to capture detailed information about your WooCommerce store's sales and revenue. This includes metrics like product performance, transaction details, and shopping behavior. Utilize this data to identify trends, make data-driven decisions, and optimize your product offerings.

Regularly analyze and interpret the data from your analytics reports to gain actionable insights. Use these insights to refine your marketing strategies, improve user experience, and drive the growth of your WooCommerce store.

By implementing Google Analytics and tracking conversions and performance metrics, you can make informed decisions based on data-driven insights. This will help you optimize your marketing efforts, enhance user experience, and drive the success of your WooCommerce store.

SECURING YOUR WOOCOMMERCE STORE

Securing your WooCommerce store is of utmost importance to protect sensitive customer information, ensure the integrity of transactions, and build trust with your audience. In this chapter, we will explore essential security measures for your WooCommerce store, including implementing SSL certificates and protecting against malware and cyber threats.

IMPLEMENTING SSL CERTIFICATES

SSL (Secure Sockets Layer) certificates encrypt the communication between your website and users' browsers, ensuring that data transmitted is secure and protected from potential eavesdropping or tampering. Here's how you can implement SSL certificates for your WooCommerce store:

Obtain an SSL Certificate: Purchase an SSL certificate from a trusted certificate authority (CA) or obtain a free SSL certificate through services like Let's Encrypt. Ensure that the certificate covers your domain name and is valid for the desired duration.

Install the SSL Certificate: The process of installing an SSL certificate may vary depending on your web hosting provider. Typically, you can install the certificate through your hosting control panel or by contacting your hosting provider's support team for assistance. Follow the instructions provided by your hosting provider to complete the installation.

Configure WordPress for HTTPS: After installing the SSL certificate, configure your WooCommerce store to use HTTPS. Update the WordPress settings by going to "Settings" > "General" and changing the URLs to include "https://" instead of "http://". Additionally, update any internal links or hardcoded URLs within your website to ensure they point to the secure HTTPS version.

Verify SSL Implementation: Test the SSL implementation by accessing your WooCommerce store using HTTPS. Check for the padlock icon in the browser's address bar, indicating a secure connection. You can also use online SSL checker tools to verify the SSL configuration and ensure everything is set up correctly.

_____ NOTE _____

If you want a comprehensive guide that explains the basics and provides a step-by-step about SSL, I recommend the book "Build a WordPress Website From Scratch 2024." This book will walk you through the entire process of setting up a WordPress website, starting from the installation phase. With detailed instructions and explanations, it will equip you with the knowledge and skills needed to create your own WordPress site.

PROTECTING AGAINST MALWARE AND CYBER THREATS

Protecting your WooCommerce store from malware and cyber threats is vital to safeguard your data and maintain the trust of your customers. Here are some measures to consider:

Keep WordPress and Plugins Updated: Regularly update WordPress, themes, and plugins to ensure you have the latest security patches and bug fixes. Outdated software can be vulnerable to exploits, making it essential to stay up to date with the latest releases.

Use Strong and Unique Passwords: Use strong, complex passwords for all user accounts associated with your WooCommerce store, including admin accounts, FTP, and hosting accounts. Avoid using common passwords and consider utilizing password management tools to generate and store strong passwords securely.

Employ Security Plugins: Install reputable security plugins specifically designed for WooCommerce stores. These plugins offer features like malware scanning, firewall protection, login protection, and brute-force attack prevention. Some popular security plugins include Wordfence, Sucuri, and iThemes Security.

Enable Two-Factor Authentication: Implement two-factor authentication (2FA) for additional security. With 2FA, users are required to provide a second verification method, such as a unique code sent to their mobile device, along with their password, adding an extra layer of protection against unauthorized access.

Regularly Back Up Your Website: Perform regular backups of your WooCommerce store to ensure that you have a recent copy of your data in case of any security incidents or data loss. Store backups securely in offsite locations or utilize backup services provided by your hosting provider.

Monitor for Suspicious Activity: Stay vigilant and monitor your WooCommerce store for any unusual or suspicious activity. Use security monitoring tools or services that provide alerts for potential security breaches, unauthorized logins, or suspicious file modifications.

Implementing SSL certificates and employing robust security measures will help protect your WooCommerce store from potential threats, ensure the safety of customer data, and enhance trust in your online business. Regularly review and update your security practices to stay ahead of evolving security risks and maintain a secure shopping environment for your customers.

CREATING A USER-FRIENDLY CHECKOUT PROCESS

Creating a user-friendly checkout process is essential for ensuring a smooth and seamless shopping experience for your customers. In this chapter, we will explore strategies to simplify the checkout steps, implement guest checkout, and provide user registration options to enhance the usability of your WooCommerce store.

SIMPLIFYING CHECKOUT STEPS

A lengthy and complicated checkout process can lead to cart abandonment and frustrate customers. Streamlining the checkout steps can significantly improve the user experience and increase conversion rates. Consider the following tips to simplify the checkout process:

Minimize Required Information: Only ask for essential information during checkout. Requesting too much unnecessary information can overwhelm customers and make the process feel tedious. Stick to the basics, such as billing/shipping addresses, contact details, and payment information.

Use a Single-Page Checkout: Consider implementing a single-page checkout where customers can view and complete all necessary fields on a single page. This eliminates the need for multiple page reloads and makes the process more intuitive and efficient.

Enable Auto-Fill and Address Suggestions: Implement auto-fill functionality for form fields to make it easier for customers to enter their information. Additionally, integrate address suggestion APIs like Google Places to provide accurate and quick address suggestions, reducing the need for manual input.

Provide Clear Progress Indicators: Display clear progress indicators during checkout to inform customers about the steps involved and how far they have progressed. This helps manage expectations and reduces the perception of a lengthy process.

Offer Multiple Payment Options: Provide a variety of payment options to accommodate customer preferences. Accept major credit/debit cards, digital wallets, and popular payment gateways to ensure convenience and flexibility during checkout.

_____ NOTE _____

In some countries you need to add extra fields, for example, in a Brazilian Store you need to add CPF field. In Norway a PID number field.

IMPLEMENTING GUEST CHECKOUT AND USER REGISTRATION

Some customers prefer a quick and hassle-free checkout experience without the need to create an account. Offering guest checkout allows them to complete their purchase without user registration. However, providing the option for users to create an account can have its advantages, such as easier order tracking and faster future checkouts. Consider the following strategies:

Guest Checkout: Make guest checkout prominently visible and easily accessible on the checkout page. Clearly communicate the benefits, such as faster checkout and no account creation required. Keep the required information minimal to encourage guest checkout.

User Registration: For customers who wish to create an account, offer a user registration option during checkout. Clearly explain the benefits, such as order history, saved addresses, and exclusive offers. Make the registration process quick and straightforward, with an option to create a password or use social login methods for added convenience.

Optional Account Creation: Provide the option for customers to create an account after completing their purchase as a way to simplify the checkout process. Offer incentives, such as discounts or rewards, for creating an account to encourage customer engagement.

Account Recovery and Password Reset: Ensure that the process of recovering an account or resetting passwords is user-friendly. Provide clear instructions and easily accessible links to reset passwords or retrieve account information in case customers forget their login details.

By simplifying the checkout steps, offering guest checkout, and providing user registration options, you can cater to the preferences of different customers and create a user-friendly checkout process that encourages conversions and enhances customer satisfaction.

Remember to regularly test and optimize your checkout process based on customer feedback and behavior to continually improve the usability of your WooCommerce store's checkout system.

IMPLEMENTING DISCOUNTS AND COUPONS

Implementing discounts and coupons is a powerful strategy to attract customers, drive sales, and foster customer loyalty in your WooCommerce store. In this chapter, we will explore the process of creating discount codes and promotions, as well as applying discounts to products and the shopping cart.

CREATING DISCOUNT CODES AND PROMOTIONS

Discount codes and promotions provide incentives for customers to make purchases by offering them savings on their orders. Here's how you can create and manage discount codes and promotions in WooCommerce:

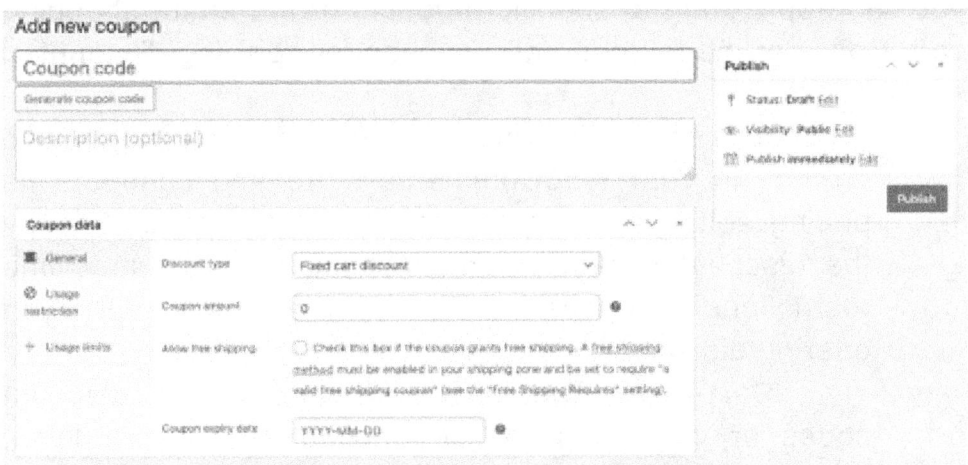

Define Your Discount Strategy: Determine the type of discount or promotion you want to offer. This could include percentage-based discounts, fixed amount discounts, buy one get one (BOGO) offers, free shipping, or bundled product deals. Align your discount strategy with your marketing goals and target audience.

Set Up Discount Codes: Access the WooCommerce dashboard and navigate to the Coupons section. Create a new coupon and configure its settings, such as the discount type, coupon amount, usage restrictions, and expiration date. Assign a unique coupon code that customers can apply during checkout to redeem the discount.

Create Promotions: WooCommerce provides options to create various types of promotions, such as scheduled sales events, discounted product bundles, or quantity-based discounts. Utilize the available promotion features to create compelling offers that align with your marketing objectives.

APPLYING DISCOUNTS TO PRODUCTS AND CART

Once you have set up your discount codes and promotions, you can apply them to specific products or the entire shopping cart. Consider the following approaches for applying discounts:

Individual Product Discounts: Edit a specific product in your WooCommerce store and configure its pricing settings to reflect the discounted price. Specify the discounted regular price, sale price, and any time restrictions if applicable. This approach is useful when offering discounts on select products.

Cart-Level Discounts: Configure your discount codes or promotions to be applied at the cart level. Customers can enter the coupon code during checkout, and the discount will be automatically calculated and applied to the eligible products in their cart. This approach allows for flexibility and encourages customers to add more items to their cart to qualify for the discount.

Conditional Discounts: Use WooCommerce extensions or plugins to implement conditional discounts based on specific conditions, such as minimum purchase amounts, specific product combinations, customer roles, or referral sources. Conditional discounts allow you to create targeted offers tailored to specific customer segments or purchase behaviors.

Tiered Discounts: Implement tiered pricing or bulk discounts to incentivize customers to purchase larger quantities of products. For example, you can offer a discount for purchasing three or more items of the same product or provide volume-based discounts based on the total quantity ordered.

By effectively implementing discounts and coupons in your WooCommerce store, you can attract customers, boost sales, and encourage repeat purchases. Regularly evaluate the performance of your discounts and promotions to optimize their impact and ensure they align with your business objectives.

Remember to communicate your discounts and promotions effectively through your website, email marketing campaigns, social media channels, and other marketing channels to maximize their visibility and reach.

MANAGING CUSTOMER REVIEWS AND RATINGS

Customer reviews and ratings play a crucial role in building trust, influencing purchase decisions, and enhancing the credibility of your WooCommerce store. In this chapter, we will explore how to effectively manage customer reviews and ratings, enabling you to leverage them as a valuable asset for your business.

ENABLING AND MODERATING CUSTOMER REVIEWS

Enable Customer Reviews: In WooCommerce, you can enable customer reviews for your products, allowing customers to share their experiences and opinions. Navigate to the WooCommerce settings and ensure that the "Enable reviews" option is checked. This will enable the review functionality on your product pages.

Moderation Settings: It's important to set up moderation controls to maintain the quality and integrity of customer reviews. Configure moderation settings to manually approve reviews before they appear on your website. This allows you to review and filter out any inappropriate or spammy content.

Review Guidelines: Establish clear guidelines for customers regarding the type of feedback they can provide. Communicate your expectations regarding constructive criticism, respectful language, and relevant content. Display these guidelines on your website to encourage customers to leave helpful and informative reviews.

Responding to Reviews: Actively engage with customer reviews by responding to them in a timely manner. Address any concerns or issues raised by customers and express appreciation for positive feedback. Responding to reviews demonstrates your commitment to customer satisfaction and encourages ongoing engagement.

ENCOURAGING POSITIVE REVIEWS AND RATINGS

Provide Outstanding Customer Service: Deliver exceptional customer service experiences to increase the likelihood of positive reviews. Respond promptly to customer inquiries, resolve any issues efficiently, and go above and beyond to exceed customer expectations. Happy customers are more likely to leave positive reviews.

Follow-Up Emails: Send follow-up emails to customers after their purchase, thanking them for their business and kindly requesting feedback. Include links to your product review pages, making it convenient for customers to leave reviews. Personalize the emails to create a more genuine connection with your customers.

Incentivize Reviews: Offer incentives, such as discounts, loyalty points, or exclusive access to content, to customers who leave reviews. However, ensure that these incentives do not compromise the authenticity of the reviews. Encourage customers to provide honest feedback to maintain the credibility of your review system.

Showcase Positive Reviews: Highlight positive reviews and testimonials on your website, product pages, or landing pages. This social proof helps build trust with potential customers and encourages them to make a purchase. Consider using review plugins or widgets to display customer reviews prominently.

Regularly monitor and analyze customer reviews and ratings to gain insights into customer satisfaction, product improvements, and areas of excellence. Use this feedback to continuously enhance your products and services, demonstrating your commitment to delivering exceptional customer experiences.

By enabling and moderating customer reviews, responding to feedback, and encouraging positive reviews, you can harness the power of customer testimonials to build a strong reputation, attract new customers, and foster long-term relationships with your audience. Remember, transparency and authenticity are key when managing customer reviews, as they contribute to the overall credibility and success of your WooCommerce store.

UTILIZING MARKETING AND PROMOTIONAL TOOLS

Marketing and promotional strategies are essential for driving sales and growing your WooCommerce store. In this chapter, we will explore key tools and techniques to enhance your marketing efforts and maximize your promotional opportunities.

EMAIL MARKETING INTEGRATION

Choose an Email Marketing Platform: Select an email marketing platform that integrates seamlessly with WooCommerce. Popular options include Mailchimp, Constant Contact, and Klaviyo. These platforms allow you to create targeted email campaigns, automate customer communication, and track the effectiveness of your marketing efforts.

Sync Customer Data: Integrate your email marketing platform with WooCommerce to synchronize customer data. This includes customer email addresses, purchase history, and other relevant information. By having accurate and up-to-date customer data, you can personalize your email campaigns and deliver relevant content to your audience.

Abandoned Cart Recovery: Implement abandoned cart recovery emails to remind customers about the products they left in their carts. Use enticing subject lines, personalized content, and special offers to encourage customers to complete their purchase. This strategy helps recover potentially lost sales and boosts your conversion rates.

Segmented Email Campaigns: Leverage customer segmentation to send targeted and personalized email campaigns. Segment your customer base based on their purchase history, preferences, or demographics. This allows you to tailor your messaging and promotions to specific customer groups, increasing the likelihood of engagement and conversion.

IMPLEMENTING UPSELLING AND CROSS-SELLING TECHNIQUES

Upselling Strategies: Utilize upselling techniques to encourage customers to upgrade to higher-priced or more feature-rich products. Display related products or product bundles that offer enhanced value or additional benefits. Highlight the advantages and justify the price difference to convince customers to make an upgraded purchase.

Cross-Selling Techniques: Cross-selling involves recommending complementary products or accessories that enhance the customer's original purchase. Display related products on product pages or during the checkout process to encourage customers to add more items to their cart. Present these recommendations as valuable additions that enhance their overall experience.

Product Recommendations: Utilize product recommendation plugins or tools to dynamically suggest relevant products based on customer browsing or purchase history. Display these recommendations on product pages or in personalized email campaigns. This strategy encourages customers to explore additional products that align with their interests and preferences.

Limited-Time Promotions: Create a sense of

urgency and exclusivity by offering limited-time promotions or discounts. Use countdown timers, limited stock notifications, or flash sales to encourage customers to take immediate action. These tactics create a sense of urgency and drive conversions by capitalizing on customers' fear of missing out.

Regularly monitor and analyze the performance of your marketing and promotional efforts. Track key metrics such as open rates, click-through rates, conversion rates, and revenue generated from email campaigns and upselling techniques. This data will help you refine your strategies and optimize your marketing initiatives for better results.

By integrating email marketing, implementing upselling and cross-selling techniques, and leveraging marketing tools, you can effectively promote your products, drive customer engagement, and increase your sales revenue. These strategies empower you to build strong relationships with your customers and maximize the potential of your WooCommerce store.

INTEGRATING SOCIAL MEDIA AND SHARING FEATURES

In today's digital age, leveraging the power of social media is essential for the success of your WooCommerce store. In this chapter, we will explore how to integrate social media platforms and implement social sharing features to enhance your store's reach and engagement.

CONNECTING YOUR WOOCOMMERCE STORE TO SOCIAL MEDIA PLATFORMS

To expand your store's visibility and connect with your audience, it's crucial to integrate your WooCommerce store with popular social media platforms. Here are the steps to follow:

Create Business Accounts: Set up dedicated business accounts on social media platforms such as Facebook, Instagram, Twitter, Pinterest, and LinkedIn.

Link Social Media Profiles: In your WooCommerce store settings, find the social media integration options. Connect your store to your social media profiles by entering the respective account details or integrating with social media plugins.

Add Social Media Icons: Place social media icons prominently on your website, preferably in the header or footer section. These icons will link to your social media profiles, allowing visitors to follow and engage with your brand on social media.

Enable Social Sharing: Enable social sharing buttons on your product pages and blog posts. This allows visitors to easily share your content on their social media accounts, extending your reach and potentially driving more traffic to your store.

ADDING SOCIAL SHARING BUTTONS

Social sharing buttons are a powerful tool to encourage your customers to share your products and content on their social media networks. Here's how to incorporate social sharing buttons into your WooCommerce store:

Choose a Social Sharing Plugin: There are several social sharing plugins available for WooCommerce. Research and select a plugin that suits your needs, ensuring compatibility with your theme and desired social media platforms.

Install and Configure the Plugin: Install the selected social sharing plugin from the WordPress plugin directory or a trusted third-party source. Follow the plugin's documentation to configure it according to your preferences, such as button placement, style, and available social media platforms.

Customize Button Placement: Determine where you want the social sharing buttons to appear on your product pages and blog posts. Common options include above or below the content, floating sidebars, or pop-up overlays.

Select Social Media Platforms: Choose the social media platforms you want to include in your sharing buttons. The most popular options are Facebook, Twitter, Instagram, Pinterest, and LinkedIn. Consider your target audience and the platforms they are most active on.

Test and Optimize: After adding social sharing

buttons, thoroughly test their functionality across different devices and browsers. Monitor their usage and analyze which platforms generate the most engagement. Use this data to optimize your social media marketing strategy.

By integrating social media platforms and implementing social sharing buttons, you can amplify the reach of your WooCommerce store, increase brand awareness, and encourage user-generated promotion. Embrace the power of social media to engage with your audience and drive more traffic to your store.

SCALING AND GROWING YOUR WOOCOMMERCE STORE

Congratulations on successfully launching your WooCommerce store! In this chapter, we will explore strategies to scale and grow your online business, allowing you to reach a wider audience and maximize your revenue potential.

OPTIMIZING PERFORMANCE FOR HIGH TRAFFIC

As your WooCommerce store gains popularity, it's crucial to ensure that it can handle increased traffic and deliver a seamless user experience. Here are some tips to optimize your store's performance:

Choose a Reliable Hosting Provider: Evaluate your current hosting plan and consider upgrading to a more robust solution that can accommodate higher traffic volumes. Look for providers that offer dedicated hosting, cloud hosting, or managed WooCommerce hosting, as they are designed to handle increased demands.

Implement Caching: Enable caching mechanisms to speed up your store's performance. Caching plugins, such as WP Rocket or W3 Total Cache, can generate static versions of your pages, reducing the server load and improving response times for visitors.

W3 Total Cache is a popular WordPress plugin that improves the performance and speed of your website by implementing various caching techniques. Caching helps reduce the load on your server, decreases page load times, and improves overall user experience. Here's an overview of what W3 Total Cache does:

Page Caching: The plugin generates static HTML files of your dynamic WordPress pages, which are then served to visitors instead of processing the heavier PHP scripts every time. This results in faster page loading times.

Browser Caching: W3 Total Cache instructs the user's browser to store certain static files, such as CSS, JavaScript, and images, locally. When the user visits another page on your site, these files are loaded from the browser's cache instead of making additional server requests, further improving load times.

Database Caching: This feature caches database queries, reducing the number of times WordPress needs to fetch data from the database. By minimizing database interactions, your website's performance is enhanced.

Object Caching: W3 Total Cache provides object caching, which stores frequently used objects or data in memory. This reduces the processing time required to retrieve data, resulting in improved website performance.

Minification and Compression: The plugin allows you to minify and compress your CSS and JavaScript files, reducing their file size without affecting functionality. Smaller file sizes mean faster file transfers and improved page loading times.

CDN Integration: W3 Total Cache integrates with content delivery networks (CDNs) to serve static content, such as images and files, from geographically distributed servers. CDNs help deliver content faster to visitors by minimizing the physical distance between the server and the user.

Mobile Optimization: The plugin includes features for optimizing your site for mobile devices, such as responsive design support and the ability to create separate caches for mobile users.

Optimize Images: **Large image files can slow down your** website. Compress and optimize product images to reduce their file size without compromising quality. Consider using image optimization plugins like Smush or ShortPixel to automate the process.

Utilize Content Delivery Networks (CDNs): CDNs distribute your website's content across multiple servers worldwide, improving loading times for visitors in different geographical locations. Services like Cloudflare or StackPath offer CDN solutions that integrate seamlessly with WooCommerce.

EXPANDING YOUR PRODUCT RANGE AND MARKET REACH

To grow your WooCommerce store, it's essential to expand your product range and reach new markets. Here are some strategies to consider:

Research Market Trends: Stay updated with market trends and identify potential product opportunities. Conduct market research, monitor industry forums, and analyze customer feedback to determine which products are in demand.

Diversify Your Product Catalog: Expand your product offerings by introducing new products or variations of existing ones. Consider customer preferences, emerging trends, and complementary products that align with your target audience's needs and interests.

Target New Audiences: Identify niche markets or untapped customer segments that align with your products. Develop targeted marketing campaigns to reach these audiences through social media advertising, content marketing, or influencer collaborations.

Explore International Markets: Consider expanding your business internationally by offering shipping options to customers in different countries. Localize your store by providing multi-language support, accepting multiple currencies, and complying with international shipping regulations.

Collaborate with Influencers: Partner with influencers or industry experts who can promote your products to their followers. Influencer marketing can help you reach a wider audience and build trust with potential customers.

Remember to track and analyze your store's performance regularly. Utilize data from analytics tools like Google Analytics to identify areas for improvement, understand customer behavior, and make data-driven decisions.

By optimizing your store's performance for high traffic and expanding your product range and market reach, you can scale your WooCommerce store and unlock its growth potential. Stay proactive, adapt to market changes, and continuously improve the customer experience to thrive in the competitive e-commerce landscape.

TROUBLESHOOTING AND COMMON ISSUES

As with any technology, you may encounter occasional challenges while running your WooCommerce store. In this chapter, we will discuss common issues that WooCommerce users face and provide solutions to troubleshoot and resolve them effectively.

COMMON WOOCOMMERCE ISSUES AND SOLUTIONS

Payment Gateway Errors: If customers experience problems during the payment process, such as transactions not going through or error messages, ensure that your payment gateway settings are configured correctly. Verify your payment gateway credentials, check for compatibility issues with your WooCommerce version, and consult the documentation provided by your payment gateway provider for troubleshooting steps.

Shipping Calculation Errors: Incorrect shipping costs or inaccurate calculations can frustrate customers and impact your store's profitability. Double-check your shipping settings, including shipping zones, methods, and rates. Ensure that your product dimensions and weight are accurately entered. If issues persist, consider using a shipping plugin that offers more flexibility and customization options.

Theme and Plugin Conflicts: Conflicts between themes and plugins can lead to compatibility issues and unexpected behavior on your site. If you experience problems after installing or updating a theme or plugin, disable them one by one to identify the source of the conflict. Contact the theme or plugin developers for assistance or search support forums for similar issues and solutions.

Slow Loading Times: Slow loading times can drive away visitors and negatively impact your search engine rankings. Optimize your store's performance by following best practices such as caching, image optimization, and minimizing the use of unnecessary plugins. Consider using a performance monitoring tool to identify bottlenecks and optimize your site accordingly.

Database and Data Integrity Issues: Problems with your WooCommerce database can result in missing or inaccurate data, affecting order processing and customer information. Regularly back up your database and utilize database optimization plugins to maintain data integrity. If you encounter database-related errors, consult WooCommerce documentation or seek assistance from support forums or a qualified developer.

SEEKING SUPPORT AND TROUBLESHOOTING TECHNIQUES

When facing challenges with your WooCommerce store, it's essential to know where to seek support and apply effective troubleshooting techniques. Here are some steps to consider:

Consult Documentation and Knowledge Base: WooCommerce provides comprehensive documentation and a knowledge base that covers various aspects of running your store. Browse through the available resources to find answers to common issues or learn more about specific features.

Support Forums and Communities: Join WooCommerce support forums and communities where you can connect with other users and seek advice. Often, fellow users or WooCommerce experts can provide insights and solutions based on their experiences.

Contact Plugin and Theme Developers: If the issue is related to a specific plugin or theme, reach out to the respective developers for assistance. Most developers offer support channels, including email, forums, or live chat, to address user queries and troubleshoot issues.

Consider Professional Help: For complex or persistent issues that require technical expertise, consider hiring a WooCommerce developer or consultant. They can analyze your store's setup, identify the root cause of the problem, and provide tailored solutions.

Remember to document any troubleshooting steps you take, including changes made to settings or configurations. This documentation can help you track your actions and revert any changes if necessary.

With the troubleshooting techniques and solutions provided in this chapter, you'll be well-equipped to tackle common issues that may arise in your WooCommerce store. Remember to stay patient and methodical while investigating problems, and leverage the resources available to you, including documentation, support forums, and professional assistance when needed.

FINALIZING YOUR STORE AND GOING LIVE

After putting in the effort to set up and configure your WooCommerce store, it's time to finalize the details and prepare for the exciting moment of launching your online business. In this chapter, we will guide you through the crucial steps of testing, reviewing, and ultimately launching your WooCommerce store.

TESTING AND REVIEWING YOUR WEBSITE

Before making your store publicly accessible, it's important to thoroughly test and review every aspect to ensure a seamless and positive user experience. Here are some key areas to focus on:

User Experience (UX): Navigate through your website as a customer would, testing all the features and functionalities. Pay attention to the layout, responsiveness, and ease of use. Verify that links, buttons, and forms are working correctly.

Checkout Process: Test the entire checkout process from start to finish, ensuring that customers can smoothly add products to their cart, enter shipping and billing information, select payment options, and successfully complete their orders. Verify that all payment gateways are functioning properly.

Responsive Design: Test your store's responsiveness across different devices and screen sizes, including desktops, laptops, tablets, and smartphones. Ensure that your website adapts and displays correctly on each platform.

Browser Compatibility: Test your website on various web browsers such as Google Chrome, Mozilla Firefox, Safari, and Microsoft Edge to ensure consistent performance and appearance across different platforms.

Product Listings: Review all your product listings to ensure accuracy, including product descriptions, pricing, images, and inventory quantities. Remove any placeholder or test content and ensure that all products are properly categorized.

LAUNCHING YOUR WOOCOMMERCE STORE

Once you have thoroughly tested and reviewed your website, it's time to make your store live and start welcoming customers. Follow these steps to launch your WooCommerce store successfully:

Set your Store to "Live" Mode: In your WooCommerce settings, change the store status from "Maintenance" or "Coming Soon" to "Live" mode. This will make your store publicly accessible to visitors.

Double-Check Payment and Shipping Settings: Review your payment and shipping settings one last time to ensure they are configured correctly. Test the payment process using real transactions (if possible) to ensure seamless integration with your chosen payment gateway.

Enable SSL Certificate: Install and enable an SSL certificate to secure your website and customer data. This helps build trust and ensures that sensitive information, such as payment details, is encrypted during transmission.

Install Security Plugins: Enhance the security of your WooCommerce store by installing security plugins that provide protection against common threats and vulnerabilities. Regularly update these plugins to maintain a secure environment.

Notify Your Audience: Announce the launch of your WooCommerce store through various marketing channels, such as your website, social media platforms, email newsletters, and any other channels you use to engage with your audience. Encourage them to explore your products and make purchases.

Monitor and Iterate: After launching your store, closely monitor its performance, track analytics, and gather customer feedback. Continuously make improvements based on the insights you gather to enhance the user experience and drive sales.

By thoroughly testing and reviewing your website and following the steps to launch your WooCommerce store, you are ready to introduce your online business to the world. Remember to continually monitor your store's performance, address any issues promptly, and adapt to the evolving needs of your customers. With dedication and ongoing optimization, your WooCommerce store has the potential to thrive and succeed in the competitive online marketplace.

Congratulations on reaching this milestone! In the final chapter of this guide, we will provide a summary of the key takeaways and offer additional resources to support your continued success with your WooCommerce store.

FUTURE TRENDS AND TIPS FOR SUCCESS

As an online store owner, it's important to stay informed about the latest trends and continuously improve your strategies to ensure the long-term success of your WooCommerce store. In this chapter, we will explore some future developments in WooCommerce and provide valuable tips to help you grow and maintain a successful online business.

EXPLORING FUTURE DEVELOPMENTS IN WOOCOMMERCE

Mobile Commerce: With the increasing use of smartphones and tablets for online shopping, mobile commerce is a rapidly growing trend. Stay updated with responsive design practices and optimize your store for mobile devices to provide a seamless shopping experience for your mobile customers.

Voice Commerce: Voice assistants like Amazon's Alexa and Apple's Siri are becoming more prevalent in households. Consider optimizing your store for voice search and enabling voice-based purchasing to tap into this emerging market.

Artificial Intelligence (AI) and Machine Learning (ML): AI and ML technologies can provide valuable insights into customer behavior, personalize the shopping experience, and streamline various processes. Explore AI-powered solutions and automation tools to enhance your store's efficiency and customer engagement.

Social Commerce: Social media platforms are evolving into shopping destinations, with features like shoppable posts and integrated checkout options. Integrate your WooCommerce store with social media platforms to reach a wider audience and drive sales through social commerce.

TIPS FOR GROWING AND MAINTAINING A SUCCESSFUL STORE

Regularly Update and Optimize Your Store: Keep your WooCommerce store up to date with the latest software versions, security patches, and plugin updates. Regularly review and optimize your product listings, pricing, and customer experience to stay competitive in the market.

Provide Excellent Customer Service: Offer prompt and helpful customer support through multiple channels, such as live chat, email, and phone. Respond to customer inquiries and issues in a timely manner, and strive to exceed their expectations with exceptional service.

Leverage Data and Analytics: Utilize data analytics tools to gain insights into customer behavior, sales trends, and website performance. Make data-driven decisions to improve your marketing strategies, product offerings, and overall user experience.

Continuously Market and Promote Your Store: Implement effective marketing strategies to drive traffic to your store. Utilize social media marketing, content marketing, email marketing, and search engine optimization (SEO) techniques to increase your online visibility and attract potential customers.

Build Customer Loyalty: Implement a loyalty program or reward system to encourage repeat purchases and foster customer loyalty. Offer exclusive discounts, personalized recommendations, and special promotions to your loyal customers.

Stay Abreast of Industry Trends: Keep yourself updated with the latest trends, news, and best practices in the e-commerce industry. Attend industry conferences, join relevant forums and communities, and follow influential voices to stay ahead of the curve.

By staying informed about future developments in WooCommerce and implementing the tips for success, you can position your online store for growth and maintain a thriving business in the ever-evolving e-commerce landscape. Embrace emerging technologies, provide exceptional customer experiences, and continuously refine your strategies to adapt to changing customer preferences and market dynamics.

We hope this guide has provided you with valuable insights and guidance throughout your WooCommerce journey. Remember, success in e-commerce is a continuous process of learning, adapting, and innovating. Wishing you all the best in your future endeavors!

CONCLUSION

Congratulations on reaching the conclusion of this comprehensive guide to WooCommerce! Throughout this journey, we have covered various aspects of building, managing, and growing your WooCommerce store. Before we wrap up, let's recap some of the key takeaways from this guide and provide some final thoughts as you embark on your WooCommerce journey.

RECAP OF KEY TAKEAWAYS

- WooCommerce is a powerful e-commerce platform built on WordPress, offering flexibility, scalability, and a wide range of features to create and manage your online store.
- Planning is essential before starting your WooCommerce store. Define your target audience, research your niche, and strategize your product offerings and marketing approaches.
- Designing and customizing your store's appearance is crucial for creating a visually appealing and user-friendly shopping experience. Choose a WooCommerce-compatible theme, customize it to reflect your brand, and optimize it for mobile devices.
- Adding and managing products in WooCommerce involves creating simple or variable products, managing inventory, and utilizing product attributes to provide detailed information and improve searchability.
- Configuring payment gateways, shipping options,

and other essential settings ensures smooth and secure transactions for your customers.

- Marketing, SEO optimization, and integrating social media platforms are vital for driving traffic, increasing visibility, and expanding your customer base.

- Monitoring analytics, managing customer reviews, and providing exceptional customer service are key to understanding your audience, building trust, and fostering customer loyalty.

- As your store grows, consider scaling your operations, optimizing performance, and exploring future trends to stay competitive and meet the changing needs of your customers.

EMBARKING ON YOUR WOOCOMMERCE JOURNEY

Now that you have gained a comprehensive understanding of WooCommerce and the various aspects of running an online store, it's time to embark on your WooCommerce journey. Remember, building a successful e-commerce business takes time, effort, and continuous learning.

Start by putting into practice the knowledge you have gained from this guide. Take small steps, experiment with different strategies, and adapt based on the feedback and data you receive. Stay updated with the latest trends and industry news, and don't hesitate to seek support and guidance from the WooCommerce community and experts when needed.

Maintain a customer-centric approach throughout your journey. Focus on providing exceptional experiences, listening to customer feedback, and constantly improving your products and services.

Lastly, enjoy the process and celebrate your achievements along the way. Building and growing a WooCommerce store is an exciting and fulfilling endeavor that offers endless opportunities for success.

Best of luck as you embark on your WooCommerce journey. May your online store thrive and bring you joy and prosperity.

THE AUTHOR

Hi, I am Raphael Heide. I started the journey as a full stack and freelance designer in 2001. Working remotely or in local for agencies around the world, advising startups and collaborating with talented people to create digital products for commercial and consumer use.

I am a professional with a strong background in WordPress development, design, and cyber security. With a passion for technology and a keen interest in the web industry, I have dedicated my career to creating innovative solutions and ensuring the security of digital platforms.

WORDPRESS PLUGİNS

I have extensive experience in developing WordPress plugins. These plugins are designed to enhance the functionality and capabilities of WordPress websites, allowing users to customize their sites and add new features. I strive to create efficient and reliable plugins that contribute to the overall user experience and help website owners achieve their goals.

WEBDESİGN

Alongside plugin development, I am also proficient in web design. I believe that an aesthetically pleasing and user-friendly design plays a crucial role in the success of a website. By combining my technical expertise with a creative eye, I create visually appealing websites that effectively convey information, engage visitors, and reflect the brand identity of my clients.

CYBER SECURİTY

Given the increasing importance of online security, I have developed a strong focus on cyber security. I understand the potential threats and vulnerabilities that websites face and work diligently to implement robust security measures. From securing websites against malicious attacks to performing vulnerability assessments and providing recommendations for enhancing security, I prioritize safeguarding digital assets and ensuring data protection.

- Raphael Heide -
www.raphaelheide.com
2023